ENGLISH

COUNTRY HOUSES

OPEN TO THE PUBLIC

SYON HOUSE, MIDDLESEX: THE DRAWING-ROOM

CHRISTOPHER HUSSEY

English Country Houses

OPEN TO THE PUBLIC

Country Life Limited

Charles Scribner's Sons: New York

First published in 1951
by Country Life Limited
Tavistock Street London WC2
and in the United States of America
by Charles Scribner's Sons
597 Fifth Avenue New York 17
Printed in Great Britain by
Hazell Watson and Viney Limited
Aylesbury and London

Foreword

THESE illustrations of the principal country houses of England and Wales now open to the public are arranged chronologically. Geographical distribution is indicated in the topographical list on p. 8. The name of the owner is given at the head of each descriptive note accompanying the illustrations, and that of the occupant (if not the same) in italics. Particulars of admission, etc., are not given, but will be found, together with the exact location of each house and concise notes, in the complete alphabetical list of *Country Houses Open to the Public*, by Gordon Nares (Country Life).

The chronological order adopted here is based on recorded (or predominant) date: for instance, Penshurst Place will be found in Section 2, *Manor Houses*, 1300–1500; but Knole, though dating originally from that epoch, is placed in Section 5, *Jacobean Mansions*, 1600–1650, in view of the predominance of that period in its existing character. These descriptive subdivisions, to be found in the List of Contents and also printed at the head of the facing pages in the text, are for the convenience of readers who may be interested in a particular historical phase. As further guide for intending visitors, on p. 10 are given lists of country houses:

1. Now used as museums or picture galleries.
2. Containing notable private collections of (*a*) paintings, (*b*) furniture, (*c*) historical interest.
3. Having good gardens and parks.

The historical notes, whilst briefly expanding these references to contents, etc., explain shortly the architectural evolution of country houses, and the social, economic, and other influences affecting their design. Indeed, the country houses now accessible form a continuous series illustrating every important stage in this aspect of national history.

Contents

I. CASTLES AND ABBEYS, 1066–1500

II. MANOR HOUSES, 1300–1500

III. TUDOR HOMES, 1500–1600

IV. ELIZABETHAN RENAISSANCE, 1550–1600

V. JACOBEAN MANSIONS, 1600–1650

VI. LATE STUART, 1650–1700

VII. THE GOLDEN AGE, 1700–1760

VIII. THE AGE OF ELEGANCE, 1760–1800

IX. NINETEENTH AND TWENTIETH CENTURIES

ILLUSTRATIONS are from *Country Life* photographs, with the exception of the following to whom acknowledgement is made : Graphic Photo Union, Plates 2, 177 ; Aerofilms, 3, 4, 22 ; F. Frith & Co., 9 ; Kenneth Shepherd, 25 ; A. F. Kersting, A.I.B.P., F.R.P.S., 37, 38, 40, 105, 147, 149, 150, 168, 169, 234 ; National Buildings Record, 44 ; J. Dixon-Scott, 49 ; Eric Guy, 51 ; Corporation of Ipswich, 69 ; Topical Press, 78 ; The British Council, 116 ; Director, Temple Newsam House, 119, 120 ; City of Birmingham, 121, 122 ; Raphael Tuck & Sons, 123 ; Valentine & Sons, 129 ; H. Moore, 130 ; E. S. B. Elcome, 151 ; *The Times*, 155, 202 ; British Railways, 161 ; Planet News, 167, 170 ; Bennett Clark, 248.

Topographical List

Museums, Art Collections, Gardens

I. COUNTRY HOUSES NOW PUBLIC MUSEUMS OR GALLERIES

II. COUNTRY HOUSES CONTAINING NOTABLE COLLECTIONS

III. GARDENS OR PARKS OF INTEREST

* Also outstanding collections of ceramics, textiles, and metal-work.   † Historic.   ‡ Scenic and/or botanical.

Introduction

SOME of the principal country houses of England have been accessible to visitors for at least two hundred years. Early in the 18th century the great Duke of Marlborough had to make arrangements to deal with the crowds of sightseers who flocked to Blenheim Palace even before the building was finished; and when Daniel Defoe published his *Tour through the whole of Great Britain* (1724–26) with descriptions, both inside and out, of many country houses, the custom was well established. Long before that, indeed, Queen Elizabeth was always inquisitive about her subjects' houses—which may account for the great number of beds in which she is reputed to have slept. The builder of Longleat with difficulty resisted her curiosity, until the house was in a state to receive her in 1574. And what interested a Queen also, no doubt, interested many of her subjects, so that we may assume that the game of 'house-hunting' was being played in England a century before John Evelyn set down some of its earliest surviving records in the second half of the 17th century. Indeed, the size of the larger ancient mansions is partly due to the need for their being able to accommodate guests who might not always be expected, and were apt to arrive with an extensive retinue.

Thus the opening of country houses is far from being a recent phenomenon. Though the qualification of 'to the public' introduces a certain distinction, the command to receive a State visit was the beginning of the process which led to charging a shilling a head to motor-coach parties. It is true that the tourists of the 18th century, from Celia Fiennes at its opening to Farington and Lord Torrington at its close, were essentially 'carriage folk', even if they arrived on horseback. Their visit was in the nature of a social call. But reading the travel-journals and guide-books of the age, it is clear that the owners of great houses in the 18th century recognized it as a social convention, if not a public duty, to allow respectable visitors the run of their collections of works of art, no less than of their parks and farms. The *Tours*, published by Arthur Young, later Secretary of the Board of Agriculture, in 1770, testify to this enlightened view by his inserting descriptions of the architecture and contents of important houses into his accounts of the agricultural experiments of their owners—the main purpose of his investigations. The great houses of the 18th century, together with their estates, were, in fact, esteemed both by their owners and their visitors as evidences of national prosperity and civilization. Before the formation of public museums and galleries, the very important collections of pictures, sculptures, furnishings, and other works of art brought together since the Renaissance in private houses were, of course, the only means available for the study of the arts, which their possessors fully recognized. By 1800 the interest in the arts had so far expanded that certain famous houses were thrown open to the public. There is, for example, a drawing depicting a guide taking a party of people round the 'Double Cube' room at Wilton, by Rowlandson; a guide-book to Wilton was published *c.* 1750. The State rooms at Warwick Castle have been shown for 150 years.

At about that time the growing interest in antiquity began to direct public attention to the 'romance' of neglected medieval buildings. As early as 1782 a writer expressed the hope that Haddon Hall would be maintained exactly as it was; and in *Northanger Abbey* (written in 1798) Jane Austen gently satirized an already popular cult. Thenceforward it was such places as Warwick and Arundel Castles, Knole and Penshurst, Haddon and Hardwick, that drew increasing numbers of visitors. In 1820, Samuel Rogers delighted in Haddon Hall, but dismissed Chatsworth as containing nothing but statues by Canova. Largely owing to this lack of interest in them, the great Georgian houses consequently tended no longer to open their doors. This was still the position during the latter part of the 19th century, until the scale of taxation and death duties from 1910 onwards began to render the upkeep of all large country houses from their owners' normal income a serious problem, which, since the last war and accompanying economic revolution, has become insoluble.

Foreseeing the trend of events, the National Trust, a body independent of the State and supported by its members for the preservation of land and buildings, at the instance of the late Lord Lothian (see p. 89), in 1937 obtained an Act to extend its powers to include accepting funds or properties as endowments for the maintenance of country houses transferred to its care, in which, however, the former owner and his successors might continue to reside as tenants on condition that the public are admitted on stated days. A number of houses are now accessible under this scheme, to which Wallington Hall (p. 136) was the first recruit. There are also cases in which the State has accepted a house in lieu of death duties, or, where the house has been given to the National Trust, has purchased the contents, as in the case of Ham House. A large and increasing number of houses are being opened to the public by their owners for a charge, who live in a corner or nearby, and who devote the income from entrance fees (after taxation) to the upkeep of the building.

The Government are at present considering the report of the Gowers Committee (1950) recommending certain reliefs to the owner-occupier of the more notable houses, sufficient to ensure (under proper safeguards) the maintenance and upkeep of the building, its contents and surroundings, on the principle that the living essence of a country house is lost, to the nation and to the public, if it is not lived in; and that the best agent for its preservation is its hereditary possessor. Should these recommendations be given effect, the number of houses open to the public would, no doubt, be further increased. As it is, the opportunities to enjoy this unique aspect of England are now more widely available than at any time probably since the 18th century.

'Impoverished as we have become in our time by two world wars, the old wealth and superabundance gone, the immense surpluses made in the 19th century by the Industrial Revolution and invested abroad now eroded away, the country yet retains its extraordinary wealth in houses and monuments from those earlier times'.[1] Indeed, country houses, it can be asserted, are England's most characteristic visible contribution to the riches of European civilization. England was not destined to challenge the cities of Italy and the Low Countries in artistic wealth, nor the châteaux of France and the great churches of Spain in splendour. The manifestation that these give of their people's spirit, history, and customs is most completely afforded in England by her country houses with their extraordinary variety, richness of contents, beauty of setting, and, above all, by their atmosphere of being the lived-in homes of generations: qualities which can be claimed to be no less unique. That these houses are relatively little known abroad is largely due to the great majority having hitherto continued primarily to serve their purpose of being

[1] A. L. Rowse: *The England of Elizabeth.*

family homes rather than national monuments. They have remained, and to some extent still do remain, a living element in the social fabric of the nation, uniting visibly the present with national history, and demonstrating the English ideal of how best to live.

It is the nature of this way of life, rather than æsthetic or intellectual qualities, that has shaped country houses. Almost wholly lacking the impersonal grandeur and artistic elaboration of their continental counterparts, English houses are peculiar in another quality—of close union with their scenic setting. This effect is largely the contrivance of the 18th century's vogue for landscape design, which originated in England. But it also accurately expressed an historical reality: the fact that English country houses have been created, not by a feudal or courtly aristocracy, but by the essentially middle class of territorial squires, whose interests, if not always their origins, were rooted in the land.

In this light, the English country house illustrates the outstanding peculiarity of national history, whereby the disruptive forces inherent in medieval feudal and ecclesiastical society were early subjected, first by the Crown and later by Parliament, and welded into a united nation. The last feudal magnates, with scarcely an exception, were liquidated under the Tudor dynasty, during which the power and estates of the Church were also distributed between Crown and landowners; powers, in their turn, drastically reduced by the revolutions of the 17th century and the reforms of the 19th. From 1500 the new governing class was recruited from the landowning community, often through the law or trade, so that it was not uncommon for an earl of Elizabethan times to stem from a yeoman grandfather, whilst the builders of many great Georgian mansions were self-made in the process of Britain's overseas and industrial expansion. At the other end of the scale, serfdom had all but vanished by the 15th century, and although simultaneously the beginnings of enclosure in the interests of wool-production increased the numbers of landless labourers, the poor were free to advance themselves in a generally prosperous economy without the calamities of war, and the English squirearchy were on the whole benevolent masters.

The result of these factors on English historic architecture is a notable absence of extremes and marked distinctions within its range. The feudal castle was comparatively early domesticated or replaced by a dwelling-house; palaces, restricted to kings and (nominally) bishops, differed little from subjects' houses (apart from the exceptional Blenheim—a national war memorial); and the mansions of the squires, whether ennobled or not, merge indistinguishably into smaller manor hall and yeoman's house. Indeed, the typical country house of the 16th century—the age of Palladio in Italy and of Fontainebleau in France —developed from the medieval squire's hall rather than from the feudal castle. In such Elizabethan fantasies as Wollaton (p. 69) and Hardwick (p. 73), however, conservative sentiment did mingle romantic memories of chivalry with rumours of the classical Renaissance, and these strange buildings perhaps most nearly reflect the English spirit during the age of Spenser and Shakespeare.

This adolescent vitality continued into the Jacobean age, braced by the island's mastery of the seas and new-found union. Its architectural style corresponds to that of the *quattrocento* in Italy and of France under Francis I. Maturity came late, and through the medium, not of aristocratic art as offered by the cavalier Inigo Jones, but of science. In 1665 Christopher Wren was still the young prodigy of the newly established Royal Society of scientists; but within a decade the reconstruction of London after the Fire and the re-orientation of thought begotten by Isaac Newton and his fellows, guided by Wren's genius and precedents from Holland, had established the English Renaissance idiom in building, which, with variations, has continued to the present time and is also the ancestor of the American Colonial house. Typically a rectangular brick house with sloping roofs, robust chimneys, and large, symmetrically placed windows, the beauty of the 'Queen Anne' theme lies in its liveableness and in the sensitive refinements of variation, proportions, surface treatment, and internal arrangements applied to a basically functional conception. It expressed exactly the rational, Protestant common sense that distinguished the age, and which is one, but not the only, dominant element in the English genius.

In contrast, the remarkable developments of the country house during the remainder of the 18th century were shaped by less practical but more imaginative ideals. The strangely dynamic masses of the great buildings by Vanbrugh translated the continental baroque style into terms expressing that romanticism which is inherent in the English spirit; whilst the classical purity of the 'Palladian' school, which from 1725 asserted itself in reaction to that of Wren and Vanbrugh, aimed at recreating the ideal architecture of a golden Roman age. Though the stately symmetrical houses of the Georgian era represent the late fulfilment of the classical Renaissance in England, their essentially romantic nature is revealed by the character of the surroundings in which they were set. Unlike their continental counterparts, which extended the same architectural discipline around them in formal terraces and avenues, the English classical houses stand amid scenery shaped to an ideal vision of nature derived from the Italian landscape painters of the late 17th century. The pictorial effect of, for example, Chatsworth (p. 114) or West Wycombe (p. 141) in their wooded landscapes, that recall the scenery of Claude or Poussin, is peculiar to England. The underlying cause of this transformation was the practical one that the country's agricultural system was undergoing a revolution simultaneously with the impact of classical ideals on its architecture. Consequently, scenery and buildings alike could be reshaped to conform at once to this vision of a golden age and to a more economically productive agriculture. The conception is most clearly illustrated, perhaps, in the idyllic landscape and great Palladian mansion of Stourhead (p. 128) in once barren Downland, but the same unity of architecture, park, and countryside is to be noted in almost every house of the period.

The internal design of the great Georgian country houses is more varied than their exteriors. This is notably the case with Holkham Hall (p. 132), Clandon (p. 124) and Althorp (p. 164), and is particularly characteristic of those designed by Robert Adam, whose genius carried the classical style to original heights of imagination in their interior decoration. His development can be traced from Harewood (p. 147) and Kedleston (p. 149), where Chippendale was among his collaborators, to its exquisite perfection of colouring and refinement at Osterley (p. 158) and Syon (p. 152). The work of his followers is notable at Heaton (p. 157), Buscot (p. 162), and Attingham (p. 163).

The balance of social and cultural development, of economic and productive resources, hitherto based on a primarily agricultural country, was undermined by the Industrial Revolution: that profound shift in the sources of power which, beginning in the 18th century, supported the Napoleonic war, and left its problems to the nineteenth century. In the ensuing attempts to adjust the nation's traditional ways of life and standards of value, the country house underwent curious changes of form partly inspired by a subconscious desire to re-create the past and escape from a perplexing present. To some extent this impulse had been common to every century since the Renaissance—witness the reversions to the classical past from the 16th century onwards. But whereas these in each case carried the arts of design to greater invention, the reversions of the 19th century to Gothic, Tudor, and subsequently to Queen Anne and

Georgian prototypes, while gaining something in comfort, generally failed in their design to kindle the creative flame. There is, however, considerable interest to be found by students of the period in such homes of great Victorians as Hughenden (p. 169; Disraeli) and Knebworth (p. 171; Bulwer-Lytton). Some of the best examples of the arts of the Pre-Raphaelites are to be seen at Kelmscott (p. 81), Wightwick (p. 171), Wallington (p. 136), and Buscot (p. 162).

But, consciously or unconsciously, the 19th century's taste in architecture was for the most part shaped and coloured by the principles of the picturesque—as was the 18th century's by the classic ideal. The conception, which was evolved and named as the result of the 18th century's interest in landscape, expressed a tendency always present in English art, notably in Elizabethan building and the 'romantic' baroque of Vanbrugh. The theory recognized irregularity of outline, freedom of planning, richness of texture, and harmony with setting as the chief virtues in architecture. Buildings might be in any style— Grecian, Italian, Gothic, or 'revived Tudor'—so long as they were picturesque. In this liberal attitude, and in its respect for the individual, picturesque taste reflected visually 19th-century democracy, and it is appropriate that its outstanding representation is the Houses of Parliament. The direction given by Ruskin to the Gothic revival was picturesque in origin, though his moral fervour introduced aspects of ethics and workmanship which created some confusion. The more practical William Morris, by relating the latter to building tradition and actual methods of craftsmanship, brought design back to actualities. Though Morris's direct contribution to the 20th century lies principally in the care and appreciation of old buildings, his slogan of 'fitness for purpose', joined with the immense development of 19th-century engineering, was the genesis of contemporary architecture.

The great compensating legacy of the 19th century to country houses was their gardens, in which the immense accession of plant-material was matched, as the century progressed, by the understanding with which it was applied to extensions of both the old formal and later landscape traditions. It can be said that all the renowned English gardens, even where features or their outlines go back to the 17th century, owe their existing form to the Victorian or present age. The 18th century's conception of pictorial land-scape was also revitalized by the immense accessions to horticultural resources. In the resulting modern English garden, exemplified outstandingly at Hidcote (p. 175) and Bodnant (p. 176), the formal and land-scape traditions are united, with technical expertness, so as to satisfy the requirements of the vast range of plants included as fully as the faculties of the observer.

1. Castles and Abbeys, 1066—1500

1. ARUNDEL CASTLE: THE KEEP, DRAWBRIDGE, AND BARBICAN

2. ARUNDEL CASTLE: AIR VIEW FROM THE SOUTH

Arundel Castle, Sussex. (The Duke of Norfolk.) The chief feudal stronghold of the Sussex coast, which it overlooks from the foot of the Downs. The keep, drawbridge, and barbican date in part from Earl Roger de Montgomery, soon after the Norman Conquest. The round 'shell keep'—of which the Round Tower of Windsor Castle is another example—contained the original living quarters, and represents the typical abode of a Norman baron. The castle passed to the FitzAlan Earls of Arundel in the 14th and 15th centuries, then, with much of the Mowbray inheritance, to John Howard of Norfolk, descended from Saxon Herewards and created Duke of Norfolk in 1483. The Howards played leading parts in 16th- and 17th-century history, and the castle was largely destroyed in 1649. The domestic quarters, which had grown up round the inner bailey or courtyard, have several times been rebuilt. The 15th Duke, towards the end of the last century, reconstructed them grandiosely in the style of the 13th century. The series of Howard and other portraits are notable, and there is much important 18th-century English furniture. The FitzAlan tombs in Arundel Church (15th century) are magnificent, and the downland park is among the most beautiful in England.

Cardiff Castle, Glamorganshire. (The Corporation of Cardiff.) Southern bastion of the Welsh march, and in a sense the oldest habitable castle, since the outer walls are those of a Roman fort. The *motte*, raised about 1090, carries the 13th-century keep of the de Clares, who reconstructed the whole Roman *enceinte*, and began the domestic quarters in the south-west corner. The Castle ultimately passed to the Marquesses of Bute. In the 19th century the dwelling-house was virtually rebuilt by the Victorian architect William Burges, of whose fantastic medievalism its interior is the most extraordinary example.

Raby Castle, Staindrop, Durham. (Lord Barnard.) The moated castle, licensed about 1380, was the home, from 1130 till 1569, of the senior branch of the great northern clan of Nevill, descended from Saxon thegns living hereabouts before the Norman Conquest. Since 1626 it has been the home of the Vanes, Lords Barnard, Earls of Darlington, and Dukes of Cleveland. The 14th-century kitchen survives, and there are notable Georgian rooms and contents, but much was reconstructed *c.* 1850 by William Burn.

3. CARDIFF CASTLE, INCORPORATING ROMAN, PLANTAGENET, AND VICTORIAN BUILDING

4. RABY CASTLE: SAXON ORIGINS AND 14TH-CENTURY BUILDINGS

5. ALNWICK CASTLE, ON THE RIVER ALNE

Alnwick Castle, Northumberland. (The Duke of North-umberland.) 'I never heard the old song of Percy and Douglas, that I found not my heart moved more than with a trumpet', Sir Philip Sidney confessed. The sway that the ballads of Chevy Chase and Otterburn held over the romantic imagination of Elizabethans is still excited by the sight of the ramparts and towers of the Percy stronghold. The ballad's constant if largely fictitious theme is:

> *Ther was never a tym on the march partes*
> *Sen the Doglas and the Perse met,*
> *But yt was marvele an the rede blude ronne not,*
> *As the rain does in the stret.*

Actual chronicles of the Border, confused and stirring as a vast tapestry, do give the impression of an endless chivalrous array streaming out of the gates of Alnwick, Warkworth, Bamborough, Berwick, and Norham, of Topcliff, Spofforth, Newcastle, and Prudhoe, and from as many fortresses and pele-towers north of the March, to join in continuous battle among the moorlands and bleak forests.

Holding the eastern end of the Scottish borderland, Alnwick's outer walls and keep were built in stone about 1100 by Yvo de Vesci, who succeeded its first Norman owner Gilbert Tyson, the Conqueror's standard-bearer at Hastings. During the next two centuries the castle was repeatedly but unsuccessfully be-sieged by the Scots. In 1309 the last de Vesci parted with the fief to Sir Henry Percy, of a Norman family seated in Yorkshire and Sussex, who overhauled the castle to meet Edwardian military requirements. The keep was rebuilt in the form of seven semicircular bastions round an irregular court, and the gate-towers to the outer and second baileys, with the curtain walls, assumed their present form. But the strongly fortified barbican, giving entry from the town, dates from the time of Henry, 2nd Earl of Northumberland (1414–55), son of that 'Harry Hotspur' in whom Shakespeare typified these vigorous and turbulent border chieftains. Under the Tudors and Stuarts, 'the Mag-nificent', the 'Unthrifty', and 'the Wizard' Earls successively upheld or opposed the Crown, till the Earldom became extinct in 1670.

Through two heiresses the Percy name and the bulk of the vast Percy domains eventually passed to Sir Hugh Smithson, in 1750 created Duke of Northumberland, who employed Robert Adam to make habitable rooms in the keep. But little of the Georgian work survived the effective, if drastic, restoration of the whole mass of buildings for the 4th Duke by Anthony Salvin, assisted by a team of Italian decorators and a school of local carvers. Most of the Percy family portraits are at Syon (p. 152) or Albury (p. 110), but the impressive apartments at Alnwick contain notable Italian and other paintings with some Adam and Chippendale furniture.

6. ALNWICK CASTLE: THE GATEWAY TO THE KEEP, c. 1350

7. ALNWICK CASTLE: THE STONE GARRISON OF THE BARBICAN

8. THE STATE DINING-ROOM

9. WARWICK CASTLE, ACROSS THE RIVER AVON

Warwick Castle. (The Earl of Warwick.) Surmounting a cliff above Shakespeare's Avon and commanding the still partly walled town, this beautiful and historic castle is also one of the most authentically medieval, consisting mainly of a 14th- and 15th-century *enceinte*, within which is a sumptuous 17th-century dwelling. But Ethelfleda's Mount traditionally preserves the site of the earliest stronghold erected by King Alfred's daughter, and a strong Norman castle was held throughout the earlier centuries by reliable adherents of the medieval kings. The special feature of Warwick is its lofty towers, 'Guy's', 'Cæsar's', and the formidable gatehouse, built in the 14th century by the great Beauchamp Earls of Warwick, who loom large in late medieval history. They were succeeded by Richard Nevill, Earl of Warwick, 'The King Maker' (a younger branch of the Nevills of Raby, p. 18). After a break in the succession, castle and earldom passed under Henry VIII to Robert Dudley, usurping Duke of Northumberland, beheaded 1552. Recovered by the Crown, the castle was bestowed by James I on Sir Fulke Greville, of a line of Cotswold wool merchants, created Lord Brooke, whose descendants received the earldom in 1759. The great rooms are in the 14th-century range above the river and have been open to the public for nearly 150 years. They were magnificently adorned in the second half of the 17th and enriched in the 18th century. The great hall, burnt and rebuilt in 1870, contains the mythical Guy of Warwick's 'porridge pot', Oliver Cromwell's helmet, and Izaak Walton's chest. The Red Drawing-room, with notable paintings by Velasquez, Rubens, and Vandyck, leads into the Cedar Room, the finest of the apartments, hung with Vandyck's portraits of Cavalier leaders—although the Lord Brooke of the time held Warwick for the Parliament. Other artists well represented are Holbein, Moroni, and Canaletto. The Little Boudoir and Queen Anne's Room, with lofty four-poster bed of the period, are beautiful examples of the Restoration style, with contemporary tapestries and furnishings.

10. WARWICK CASTLE: QUEEN ANNE'S ROOM

11. WARWICK CASTLE: THE CEDAR ROOM

12. CHIRK CASTLE, HILL-TOP STRONGHOLD ON THE WELSH BORDER

Chirk Castle, Denbighshire. (Colonel R. E. Myddelton.) When Edward I annexed the minor principalities of northern Powys from the Welsh confederation, he gave the section of them lying south of the River Dee to Roger Mortimer, of that turbulent line of Welsh border barons who held Ludlow and Wigmore and ultimately ascended the throne in the person of Edward IV. The castle was built in 1310 on a hill-top site which already carried some kind of primitive stronghold, and is a complete square Edwardian castle, with huge drum towers at the angles, and a square courtyard. The long, steep approach up the hill winds beneath the squat but massive towers, then passes between two more into the court, which has something of the character of a college quadrangle, for it is surrounded by the domestic quarters. These now have Elizabethan mullioned windows, inserted in 1595, when the Lordship was bought by Sir Thomas Myddelton, merchant-adventurer and backer of Sir Walter Raleigh's American voyages. His son commanded the local Parliamentary forces in the Civil War, till the tyrannical nature of the new régime converted him to Royalism. Chirk, damaged in consequence by both parties, required much repair after 1660. The State rooms were again redecorated in the Adam style 1763–73, and further alterations were made by Pugin, 1835, but without detracting from the character of the medieval structure. Besides interesting 17th-century portraits, the collection comprises landscapes by Wootton, Tillemans, and Wilson, and fine Mortlake tapestries. The old servants' hall survives intact, with curious portraits and furnishings of the 18th century. Magnificent 18th-century wrought-iron gates admit to the park, and the gardens command superb views.

13. PANELLING OF 1680 IN THE LONG GALLERY

14. ST MICHAEL'S MOUNT: THE SEA-WARD SIDE

St Michael's Mount, Cornwall. (Lord St Levan.) On the sea-girt rock lying off Marazion, Edward the Confessor founded a monastery in 1040, which was annexed to the abbey of Mont St Michel in Normandy, and from 1190, owing to its tactical strength, was combined with a royal castle. The fortress-shrine was several times captured—in 1473 by Lancastrian invaders disguised as pilgrims, in 1493 by Perkin Warbeck, who here proclaimed himself King Richard IV, but was held impregnably for the King in the Civil War. In 1660 the fortress was bought by Sir John St Aubyn, ancestor of the present owner. At high tide and during spells of stormy weather the Mount is only accessible by boat, but at low water is approached along a causeway. From its little harbour a steep and rocky path climbs through wind-cropped trees to the West Battery which guards the entrance: a granite portal in a wall dating mostly from the 16th century. The buildings, which lie round an inner court, have been much remodelled in the course of nine chequered centuries, last in 1878; but the monastic church, of which the tower is surmounted by 'St Michael's chair', crowns the rock; the 14th-century refectory is now 'Chevy Chase Hall', so-called from its plaster hunting frieze (c. 1660); and St Mary's chapel is a pretty 18th-century drawing-room containing contemporary furniture and paintings. Hydrangeas, agapanthus, and mesembryanthemum thrive on sheltered slopes of the crag.

15. THE CHEVY CHASE HALL

16. LACOCK ABBEY: 13TH- AND 16TH-CENTURY

Lacock Abbey, Wiltshire. (The National Trust; *Miss Talbot*.) Sir William Sharington, a man of the Tudor Renaissance, preserved the entire cloister (13th and 15th centuries) of the nunnery which, *c.* 1550, he converted into a highly picturesque dwelling. Sharington, servant of Protector Somerset, was a pioneer, with Sir John Thynne of Longleat (p. 67), in the new Italian architecture, and his work here comprises some of its most notable early developments in England. Georgian Gothic remodelling of the Abbess's Hall by Ivory Talbot (1753) contributes further to the romantic beauty of the home of Fox-Talbot, the pioneer of photography.

Newstead Abbey, Nottingham. (The Corporation of Nottingham.) Byron wrote of Newstead, his family home, that it 'spoke more of the baron than the monk'. Yet the noble 13th-century west end survives of the Priory Church, founded by Henry II in expiation of Becket's murder, and the Tudor mansion of Sir John Byron (1540) incorporates its cloister, refectory (now saloon with Jacobean plasterwork), and vaulted 'Guest Chamber'. In the noble terraced gardens the poet's dog 'Boatswain' is buried beneath a graceful tomb (on the site of the high altar of the church) which Byron intended to share.

17. NEWSTEAD ABBEY: THE TUDOR FOUNTAIN IN THE CLOISTER COURT

18. FLAXLEY ABBEY, IN ITS WELSH BORDER LANDSCAPE

Flaxley Abbey, Newnham, Gloucestershire. (Sir Lance Crawley-Boevey, Bt.) A Cistercian house founded in 1148 on the edge of the Forest of Dean, in memory of an Earl of Hereford killed hunting in the valley. Refectory and abbot's guest room (14th century) survive, but the 16th-century remodelling by the Kingston family predominates, adorned by Georgian work of the Boeveys, who bought the property in 1648. These (1777) comprise handsome rooms in the Adam style, and contain decorative hunting scenes by Wootton among other interesting paintings.

Beeleigh Abbey, Maldon, Essex. (Mr. W. A. Foyle.) A corner only of the cloister, 12th and 13th century, survives of this once important abbey near the old seaport. But that corner is rich in its texture of flint and mellow brickwork, and contains the vaulted chapter house and dormitory which Sir John Gale, purchaser of the Abbey at the Dissolution, adapted with little alteration to his dwelling. An interesting collection of books and manuscripts is displayed.

19. BEELEIGH ABBEY: AN EAST ANGLIAN CLOISTER

20. LUMLEY CASTLE

Towers and battlements it sees
Bosom'd high in tufted trees.

Lumley Castle, Durham. (The University of Durham.) Holding a stretch of the Great North Road, Lumley was built by Ralph, Lord Lumley, in 1389, and no castle better fulfils the idea of one than Lumley as seen looming over the grandly timbered park. Over the gates are carved the shields of Gray, Hilton, Percy, and Nevill—Lord Lumley's brothers-in-arms. Yet its interest in the evolution of the country house lies in its plan, a more civilized development from that of, for example,

Chirk (p. 26). The square court, with strong corner towers and gateway, is surrounded by living-rooms—the whole obviously transitional from castle to house. The domestic element is emphasized by the alterations made under Queen Elizabeth, and by Sir John Vanbrugh under George I. The great hall, opposite the gateway, is now chiefly of the former period, the dining-room and banqueting hall of the Georgian. In the hall is a huge equestrian effigy of Liulph, the reputed founder of the Lumley family, Earls of Scarborough, by whom the castle has been made over for educational purposes.

21. LUMLEY CASTLE: IN THE COURTYARD

22. NAWORTH CASTLE: THE DACRE TOWER AND GATEHOUSE ON THE LEFT

Naworth Castle, Brampton, Cumberland. (The Earl of Carlisle.) This famous border castle surmounts the promontory formed by two converging valleys—now thickly wooded, but originally bare—just south of the Roman Wall. The Dacres, 'Wardens of the Western Marches', were licensed in 1335 to build the surviving Dacre Tower and Gatehouse, and for two centuries exercised 'border justice'. In 1577, soon after the castle assumed its existing form, it went by marriage to Lord William Howard ('Belted Will'), father of the 1st Earl of Carlisle. Carefully restored after a fire in 1844 by Salvin, the hall and gallery contain notable tapestries and pictures.

Skipton Castle, Yorkshire. (Lord Hothfield.) Occupies a somewhat similar site to Naworth, and was a castle of the Dacres' rivals, the Lords Clifford. The 14th-century donjon encloses the picturesque Conduit Court, reconstructed under Henry VIII. Besieged and damaged in the Civil War, Skipton was one of the castles restored (1650) by the famous Lady Anne Clifford, from whom the present owner descends.

23. SKIPTON CASTLE: THE CONDUIT COURT

24. LINDISFARNE CASTLE ON HOLY ISLAND

Lindisfarne Castle, Northumberland. (The National Trust.) A fort built in 1549 against the Scots. Its beauty today is due to the turning of the ruin, which it had become in 1900, into a little 'dream castle' by Sir Edwin Lutyens.

Sizergh Castle, Kendal, Westmorland. (The National Trust; *Capt and Mrs Hornyold-Strickland.*) The home of the Strickland family for seven hundred years, the oldest part is the typical north-country pele-tower (14th century). The great hall beside the tower was reconstructed and the wings added in the 16th century; the apartments were elaborately decorated 1558–75. Of that epoch was the great chamber, of which the unusually rich panelling is now in the Victoria and Albert Museum. The room retains its elaborate ceiling, and is now hung with 17th-century Flemish tapestry; others are still finely panelled, and have very ornate over-mantels dated 1563 and 1575. The family long remained loyal to the exiled Stuarts, attending their court at Versailles. But later in the 18th century some renovation of the ancient house was possible. Of the furnishings, that of the hall (early 16th century) is remarkable; excellent silver and china of the 18th century are also to be seen.

25. SIZERGH CASTLE: THE TOWER AND FORECOURT

MEDIEVAL manor houses nearly all follow a standardized functional pattern common to most medieval houses. In the centre is the hall, used till the mid-16th century for meals in common and for manorial court meetings. Entrance is by a porch to one end, and originally the hearth was in the middle of the floor, the smoke escaping through a louvre in the roof and the unglazed windows. Kitchen, offices, and family bedrooms adjoined the hall at one end; the ladies' retiring-room or 'solar' at the other, usually with the beer cellar and storeroom beneath it. This traditional arrangement (the 'hall-house') had developed by 1300 from earlier and pre-Conquest usage, and was only defensible—by a moat and gatehouse—against casual intruders. A less common alternative type, derived from the defensible tower, takes the form of three or more rooms raised on vaulted cellars and accessible by an external removable stair: Boothby Pagnell, Lincolnshire (12th century), and Little Wenham (p. 35) represent this. Manor houses of the predominant type have in most cases, of course, been much altered subsequently.

26. BROUGHTON CASTLE: THE MOAT AND GATEHOUSE

Broughton Castle, Banbury, Oxfordshire. (Lord Saye and Sele.) Continuously inhabited since about 1340, and not licensed to be fortified until 1405, Broughton is primarily a large manor house of the early 14th century, with Elizabethan additions and decorations (1599). Bishop William of Wykeham bought Broughton in 1377 to establish a great-nephew. He was followed by the Fiennes family, its owners ever since. Early Renaissance work of 1550 and very fine Jacobean decoration is due to them. At the top of the house is the 'council chamber', where the 1st Lord Saye and Sele and his son, the Parliamentary leaders of Northamptonshire, used to confer with Hampden and Pym, in preparation for the Civil War.

27. STOKESAY CASTLE AND CHURCH

Stokesay Castle, near Ludlow, Shropshire. (Lady Magnus.) In this romantic fortified manor house the development summarized in connection with Broughton can be traced from the 12th century. At the north end the tower, surmounted by later overhanging timber-work, is part of a tower-house of Henry II's reign. It is adjoined by an unaltered great hall and solar of the 13th century, to which the prominent south tower was added by licence in 1291. The owner then was Lawrence of Ludlow, son of a celebrated wool-merchant and financier of Edward I. About 1570, a gatehouse and other alterations were made in the richly carved timber-work of this region. Defended only by a moat, the small garrison prudently surrendered in the Civil War, so that this precious document, well cared for by successive owners who long ago ceased to inhabit it, remains intact.

Little Wenham Hall, Ipswich, Suffolk. (Major A. T. C. Binny.) The home of a knight of Edward I's time, and the most notable intact survivor of the tower-house type of manor house. Built about 1270, it is also remarkable in being of brick, brownish in colour and probably imported from Flanders, since bricks were not made in England till the 15th century. The hall, above vaulted cellars, is reached by an outside wooden stair, and opens into a beautiful little chapel. Above was the sleeping-room. Kitchen and outbuildings were grouped around a small court which no longer exists.

28. LITTLE WENHAM HALL: A MANOR HOUSE OF 1270

Haddon Hall, Rowsley, Derbyshire. (The Duke
of Rutland.) Justly famed as the *beau ideal* of
historic manor houses, Haddon stands like a little
city in a medieval tapestry, the forest background
of which shrouds the semi-legendary Peveril of the
Peak, Haddon's first lord. Vernons (1170–1567)
added building to building within the 12th-century
enclosing wall, and the beautiful garden terraces
were not finished till 1650 by John Manners, later
8th Earl of Rutland, grandson of Dorothy Vernon,
whose celebrated elopement in 1567 brought
Haddon to its present possessors. The Hall owes
its perfect preservation to having never been fortified; to the prudent thrift of successive Vernons
who, though kings among their dales, aspired no
higher than knighthood; and to the late Duke of
Rutland's labour of love (1912–40) in repairing the
long-deserted home of his ancestors.

It lies round two courts, separated by the great
hall and the adjoining parlours built about 1375.
The lower court is entered beneath a lofty gate-
tower completed under Henry VIII by Sir George
Vernon, 'King of the Peak', and one side is formed

**30. THE LOWER COURT AND HALL
RANGE**

31. HADDON HALL: THE TERRACE AND LONG GALLERY

by the exquisite chapel dating from 1170 and decorated *c.* 1470. Kitchens and dining-parlour are little changed since 1500. The latter is decorated with original heraldic painting and early Tudor wainscot. The great chamber above it has rich plasterwork of 1570, and adjoins the long gallery, which was given its present form *c.* 1603. It is 110 feet long, the side to the garden almost entirely of windows, and the wall surface lined with decorative panelling grained a soft silvery grey.

A room at the end of the gallery contains a door to the garden, through which Dorothy, younger daughter of Sir George Vernon, is said to have escaped during her sister's marriage festivities in 1567, and, descending the terraces to the river, rode away with Sir John Manners. There appears to be no contemporary evidence for the tradition, however, which became current during the 19th century. But the marriages of the two heiresses did divide the great Vernon estates between the Stanley and Manners families. Sir John and Lady (Dorothy) Manners are represented on their monument in Bakewell Church.

32. MURAL DECORATION (1470) OF THE CHAPEL

33. HADDON HALL: THE HALL SCREEN, 1475

34. THE DINING-PARLOUR: PAINTED CEILING, *c.* 1500, WAINSCOT DATED 1545

35. PENSHURST PLACE FROM THE PARK

36. THE HALL RANGE (1340) AND COURTYARD

**37. PENSHURST PLACE: THE LONG GALLERY HUNG
WITH SIDNEY PORTRAITS**

Penshurst Place, Kent. (Lord De L'Isle and Dudley, V.C.)

*Thou art not, Penshurst, built to envious show . . .
But standst an ancient pile,*

Ben Jonson wrote of Sir Philip Sidney's home in 1620, then already
nearly three hundred years old. Though its chief associations are
with the Sidney family, the core of Penshurst is the great hall and
adjoining rooms built about 1340 by John de Poultney, four times
Lord Mayor of London and financier of Edward III's Crécy
campaigns. In 1393, Sir John Devereux was licensed to fortify the
house, when it was enclosed by a wall and towers, of which portions
survive. He also added a second hall, completed *c.* 1450 by Humphrey
Stafford, Duke of Buckingham, after whom it is named, and subsequently reconstructed as apartments for Queen Elizabeth. In 1552,
Penshurst was granted by Edward VI to Sir William Sidney, whose
son Sir Henry, a great Lord-Deputy of Ireland and President of
Wales, became brother-in-law of Robert Dudley, Earl of Leicester,
and was father of Sir Philip Sidney. Sir Henry added the gatehouse
1575-85, and his elder son, created Earl of Leicester in 1618, the long
gallery. Never wealthy, the Sidneys, like the Vernons of Haddon,
only adapted and added to the 'ancient pile', which has thus remained
essentially a notable and picturesque medieval mansion. Their
descendant, the 1st Lord De L'Isle and Dudley, reconstructed parts
in 1834, and his son did much to preserve the fabric, also restoring
the gardens to their Jacobean form, with the help of George Devey.

38. THE ARMOURY

39. PENSHURST PLACE: THE GREAT HALL, WITH ITS CENTRAL HEARTH

The great hall retains its central hearth and carved timber roof of the 14th century. Other rooms contain, besides the remarkable range of Sidney portraits, armour, and relics, exceptionally fine furniture of William and Mary, Kent and Chippendale periods, together with the honours awarded to Field-Marshal Lord Gort, V.C., father of Lady De L'Isle.

40. COTHELE: THE GATE TO THE COURTYARD

Cothele, Calstock, Cornwall. (The National Trust.) Family feuds long kept alive the custom of local warfare in the West Country. So when Sir Richard Edgecumbe returned with Henry Tudor (1485) to his manor beside the Tamar from which a neighbour had driven him, he rebuilt the house conservatively and strongly in granite, set round a courtyard and with a formidable gate. Thus, although quite a century later, Cothele is as medieval as Haddon Hall, and so late as 1600 a massive tower was added. Subsequently, the family moved to Mount Edgecumbe near Plymouth (destroyed by bombs in the last war), and Cothele, though uninhabited, was left unaltered as it had been in the 17th century, down to the weapons hanging on the walls of the hall. The parlours and bedrooms contain a wealth of 17th-century furniture and tapestry, which drawings made in 1840 show to have been found then almost exactly as they are now. The early Tudor chapel is no less intact, with original stained glass and woodwork. In 1840, a wing on one side of the courtyard was remodelled to provide more up-to-date accommodation, enabling thereby the remainder to be preserved unaltered. Advantage was also taken of the position of the house above a steep slope to the Tamar to create a notable garden of semi-exotic shrubs in the mild climate. The Earl of Mount Edgecumbe presented Cothele to the National Trust in 1946.

41. WINDOWS LOOKING INTO THE COURTYARD

42. COTHELE: THE GREAT HALL

In our hall is hung
Armoury of the invincible knights of old

The great hall of Cothele is an extraordinary and authentic survival of medieval usage. Completed in about 1540, it was even then old-fashioned, and has never been altered since. Its rough granite and plaster walls are hung with trophies and armour dating from the time of the Spanish Armada, though some later weapons bring its story down to the 19th century.

43. GREAT CHALFIELD MANOR

Great Chalfield Manor, Bradford-on-Avon, Wilts. (The National Trust.) Built in 1480 by Thomas Tropenell, a landowner who prudently prospered during the Wars of the Roses. Here all the components of the medieval manor house were assembled with conscious design. In the centre is the great hall, its porch balanced by its oriel window, and supported at one end by the solar wing, at the other by that containing the principal bedchamber. The kitchen offices are in the gate-house range to the west, and an elegant chapel is detached on the east side of the forecourt. In 1837, T. L. Walker, a pupil of Pugin, made careful drawings of the building which, then intact, later fell into decay till meticulously restored by Sir Harold Brakspear for Mr Robert Fuller in 1910.

Clevedon Court, Somerset. (Sir Ambrose Elton, Bt.) In the picturesque country west of Bristol. The manor-hall dates from the 14th century, and was restored at the beginning of the 18th century by the forebear of the present owner. The west wing was burnt down in 1882 and almost completely rebuilt. Clevedon Court was the model for Castlewood Hall, the home of Thackeray's Henry Esmond. Relics of the author are preserved, together with furniture and portraits of the Elton family and examples of Elton ware pottery.

44. CLEVEDON COURT

45. LYTES CARY MANOR HOUSE

Lytes Cary, Ilchester, Somerset. (The National Trust.) The home of the Lyte family from the 13th till the 18th century, the chapel (at the left-hand end of the hall range) was built about 1343, the hall—a very fine example—about 1450, and a beautiful addition, forming a quadrangle behind it, in 1533. The manor house was restored and furnished after 1907 by the late Sir Walter Jenner, Bt. The garden is laid out in alleys and lawns, with clipped hedges, in the tradition of John Lyte, a noted herbalist of Elizabethan times. The great chamber, which overlooks it, has an unusually early moulded plaster ceiling (1533), and all the rooms contain admirable 16th- and 17th-century furniture, with some early Georgian. A Life of St Joseph of Arimathea, written at Glastonbury, describes the following miracle in 1502:

> *The IX day of April, John Lyght gentylman,*
> *Dwellynge beside Ilchester at Lyghtscare,*
> *His wyfe had upon her a fever quartayn,*
> *By the space of two yere vexed greatly;*
> *No medycyne nor phisicke that could do her*
> *   remedy,*
> *She prayed to St Joseph to hele her of her payne,*
> *Then was she delyvered of her disease certayne.*

46. IN THE HALL

47. IGHTHAM MOTE: THE COURTYARD

Ightham Mote, Sevenoaks, Kent. (Sir Thomas Colyer-Fergusson, Bt.) One of the loveliest of moated houses, romantically sited in a wooded valley north of Tonbridge, and set in an old garden. The picturesque buildings, grouped round a courtyard and of many materials, comprise a very fine 14th-century hall, an early Tudor chapel, and some 17th- and 18th-century rooms. The gatehouse, through which the courtyard is entered over the moat, is of the late 15th century. The original owners were the Haut family, succeeded by Clements, Allens, and Selbys.

Stoneacre, Otham, Kent. (The National Trust.) The timber-framed hall-house of a well-to-do Kentish yeoman or small squire, John Ellys, built about 1480. In the next century an upper floor inserted in the hall obstructed the use of such a central hearth as exists at Penshurst, so a brick chimney had to be built, now containing a fine hearth of *c.* 1450. This floor was removed and the whole house restored by the late Mr Aymer Vallance, who bequeathed Stoneacre to the National Trust.

48. STONEACRE: A KENTISH YEOMAN'S HALL

49. BRADLEY MANOR

Bradley Manor, Newton Abbot, Devonshire. (The National Trust ; *Mrs Woolner*.) An interesting small manor house, its rough stone walls coated with original ochre-washed harle against the weather, was built in 1419 by Richard and Joan Yarde, the chapel at the right-hand end of the front being added in 1428. The curious oriel windows were added about 1495. Within, between hall and chapel, is a richly carved renaissance screen of about 1534.

Horton Court, Chipping Sodbury, Gloucestershire. (The National Trust.) This manor house affords an almost unique instance of a 12th-century hall. It is adjoined by a small Tudor house built about 1521 by William Knight, Secretary to Henry VII and VIII and later Bishop of Bath and Wells. The most remarkable feature is the detached 'ambulatory' or loggia built by him in perpendicular Gothic, but evidently deriving from Italian prototypes seen by him on his periodic missions to Italy.

50. HORTON COURT: A TUDOR DIPLOMAT'S LOGGIA

BEFORE the end of the 15th century, the new conception of civilization germinated in Italy had begun to transform the outlook of Englishmen. The vision of new worlds beyond the confined map of the Middle Ages, of Ancient Greece and the new America, new conceptions of man's destiny and allegiance, new ways of thought and of disseminating thought through the printed word, and new sources of wealth, begot a century of political and intellectual ferment. In England, the beginnings of this 'renaissance' coincided roughly with the Tudor dynasty's seizure of the throne (1485) and with the feudal aristocracy's eclipse by, as we should say, business men. In building, the Gothic tradition long continued, but developed a new regard for symmetry and a robust delight in ornament displaying scraps of classical 'architecture' (the word was first used about 1560). The patterns derived chiefly from Northern Europe rather than from Italy direct. Brick increasingly supplemented masonry and took the place of timber, whilst the old defensive features were retained only as decoration or were jettisoned for comfort and light. Fireplaces and chimneys multiplied; glass windows became cheaper and commoner; wainscot lined the rooms.

51. COMPTON WYNYATES: A TYPICAL EARLY TUDOR COUNTRY HOUSE

Compton Wynyates, Banbury, Warwickshire. (The Marquess of Northampton.) Compton Wynyates (meaning 'vineyard') has belonged to the Comptons since the 12th century, but was given its typical Tudor shape by William Compton, who rose to wealth as squire of the body to Henry VIII, before 1528. Originally moated, and built round a courtyard, the house is little altered. It comprises a great hall with curiously carved screen and a remarkable chapel. But it is the turreted walls of rosy brick, set in an old English garden at the foot of wooded slopes, which so picturesquely typify the period.

52. HINCHINGBROOKE : THE ENTRANCE GATEWAY, ORIGINALLY AT RAMSEY ABBEY

Hinchingbrooke, Huntingdon. (The Earl of Sandwich.) Henry VIII's dissolving of the monasteries transferred their accumulated wealth in lands and buildings to the men of the Tudor revolution. Arch-representative of these new 'managers' was the Minister mainly instrumental to the measure, Thomas Cromwell. His nephew, Richard Cromwell, in 1540 received Hinchingbrooke Nunnery, which he proceeded to convert into a quadrangular house. It is characteristic of the early Tudor reshaping of old forms to new uses that Cromwell re-erected, as his entrance gate,

a magnificent late Gothic portal brought from Ramsey Abbey, another of his spoils. Elizabethan features were added by Richard Cromwell's son Sir Henry and grandson Sir Oliver, whose nephew was that other Oliver Cromwell. But in 1627 the Cromwell connection ceased when Hinchingbrooke was bought by Sir Sidney Montagu. His son, the admiral and 1st Earl of Sandwich, was Samuel Pepys's chief and kinsman. The diarist was often here, and records many of the alterations then made, including a handsome staircase (1663) and library.

53. HINCHINGBROOKE: THE GARDEN FRONT, TUDOR AND ELIZABETHAN

A room at Hinchingbrooke is devoted to a notable assemblage of Cromwell relics and portraits, in addition to the collections of successive Earls of Sandwich. These include important seascapes and naval material connected with the 1st and 4th Earls of Sandwich, and outstanding portraits by Lely, Hogarth, Zoffany, Alan Ramsay, and the 18th-century school, with English and French furniture and needlework. Much of the house, burnt in 1834, was rebuilt at that date by Blore.

Paycockes, Great Coggeshall, Essex. (The National Trust.) No less than the courtiers and officials, industry throve under the Tudors' new order, but at the expense of the journeymen artisans and the cottage industries. Thomas Paycocke was one of the new capitalist factory owners, and in the Essex village of Coggeshall, facing the street, he built himself this house of oak and brick (*c.* 1500). Almost every beam, inside and out, is enriched with carving. On the bressummer-beam, above the male figure depicted (one of two flanking the entrance), can be descried two crowned imps shaking hands—symbolizing Henry Tudor's marriage with Elizabeth of York (**?**). Lord Noel-Buxton restored this home of his forebears and gave it to the National Trust.

54. PAYCOCKES: A DETAIL OF A TUDOR WOOL-MERCHANT'S HOUSE

55. ADLINGTON HALL: IN THE COURTYARD

Adlington Hall, Macclesfield, Cheshire. (Mrs Legh.) John de Legh, ancestor also of the Leghs of Lyme (p. 108) and Stoneleigh (p. 127), came into Adlington through marriage, *c.* 1310. His grandson commanded the Macclesfield Archers at Poitiers. About 1505 his descendant, Thomas Legh, rebuilt the hall and older portions 'after the common sort of building of the gentlemen of Lancashire and Cheshire'—that is, of oak and plaster, lying round a court and surrounded by a moat. Larger windows, chimneys, a porch, and internal comforts were introduced in 1581, and other improvements in the 17th century, culminating in the rebuilding of the outer front of the courtyard in classical brickwork in 1757. These later embellishments include handsomely panelled rooms, in which hang family portraits from Elizabethan times onwards, and the remarkable 17th-century decorations of the hall, shown on the next page, where its exceptionally interesting timber structure is described. The decorations comprise 17th-century mythological mural paintings, decorative heraldry of the Legh family's alliances from the 14th century, and the great organ with magnificently carved case installed 1740–50 in the minstrels' gallery under the supervision of Handel. He was a friend of Charles Legh, and here composed the setting of a hunting song by Mr Legh, of which the original score, signed by Handel, is preserved. It opens:

> *The Morning is charming, all Nature is gay*
> *Away, my brave Boys, to your Horses away. . . .*

56. THE GEORGIAN FRONT ADDED IN 1757

58. RUFFORD OLD HALL

57. ADLINGTON HALL

Rufford Old Hall, Southport, Lancashire. (The National Trust.) There were Heskeths since the 13th century at Rufford, where the house, built by Thomas Hesketh about 1500, contains the most completely preserved of the timber halls built in early Tudor times by the gentlemen of Lancashire and Cheshire. Rufford retains perfectly their peculiar characteristics, which at Adlington were partially obscured in the 18th century. They consist in splendid but late hammer-beam roofs (the type had been developed about 1380), a coved canopy above the dais, and, at the lower end of the hall, in

place of the continuous screen customary elsewhere (e.g. Haddon Hall, p. 38), a movable screen or 'spere' placed between massive columns supporting the roof and carved with Gothic tracery. The columns in Adlington Hall are traditionally the trunks of trees originally growing *in situ*. Between them will have stood a 'spere', such as that preserved at Rufford—the ponderous carving of which, particularly of its extraordinary pinnacles, barbarically combine late Gothic and early Renaissance motives. Rufford Old Hall was given in 1936 to the National Trust, and now houses the South Lancashire Folk Museum.

60. SUTTON PLACE

59. COUGHTON COURT

Coughton Court, Alcester, Warwickshire. (The National Trust; *Sir Robert Throckmorton, Bt.*) A castellated gatehouse was one of the medieval features inherited by Tudor mansions. That at Coughton was built in 1508 by Sir George Throckmorton on an ambitious scale which had to be modified, for the wings forming a court behind it are of Elizabethan half-timber. They contain rooms with very fine wainscot and chimney-pieces *temp.* Charles I, and historic portraits and furniture of the 17th and 18th centuries. Also, Mary Queen of Scots' nightgown, still stained crimson round the neck, is preserved in the house of a family always closely associated with the 'papist' cause.

Sutton Place, Guildford, Surrey. (The Duke of Sutherland.) A similar gatehouse, destroyed 1782, closed the court of Sutton Place, built, *c.* 1523, by Sir Richard Weston, assistant to Cardinal Wolsey and Thomas Cromwell. The building is most remarkable, in that the place of masonry is entirely taken by terra-cotta, cast in Gothic and Renaissance moulds of much delicacy by imported Italian workmen. Sir Richard Weston III (1613–52) first introduced turnips and clover to English agriculture, and financed the earliest canal—the Wey Navigation. The house is notable for the 18th-century Leveson-Gower portraits, the family of its present possessor.

61. BARRINGTON COURT: THE PERFECT EXAMPLE OF THE HENRY VIII STYLE

Barrington Court, Langport, Somerset. (The National Trust ; *Mrs Lyle.*) Barrington Court was built between 1514–20 for Lord Daubeny, a military commander who had served Henry VIII in his French war and been present at the famous pageant of the Field of the Cloth of Gold. The material is the local Ham Hill stone, of a rich golden colour, of which the quarries also produced a notable school of skilled masons. The unknown master-mason of Barrington perfected an exquisite prototype followed by English architecture for a hundred years. But the native Gothic tradition is so blended with features of the French Renaissance style that it is probable that his employer, or somebody in Lord Daubeny's household who had absorbed current developments in France, exerted considerable influence on the design. This co-ordinates all the elements of the traditional manor house into a logical and symmetrical plan—the 'E', popularly associated with Queen Elizabeth —as well as introducing one of the earliest of long galleries. In the elevations, each vertical line culminates in the sculptured finials or spiral chimneys that flower above the roof. Next to the house, and now incorporated with it, stands a brick stable quadrangle built about 1670 by the Strodes. When acquired by the Trust, the house was almost derelict, but was leased in 1920 to the late Col. A. A. Lyle, who carefully restored it, and used the rooms to display his collection of oak wainscoting.

2. THE HALL PORCH OF GOLDEN HAM HILL STONE

63. SPEKE HALL: THE ENTRANCE ACROSS THE DRY MOAT

Speke Hall, Lancashire. (The National Trust.) Another of the great black-and-white houses of the Cheshire-Lancashire gentry, now on the outskirts of Liverpool. Like Adlington, the buildings surround a courtyard, but, unlike, they are all in the same style—though not of one date. The Norris family lived at Speke as early as 1339 till 1794, and three generations of Sir William Norrises built the present house. The framework of the hall, on the farther side of the courtyard, probably dates from about 1525, and the gabled range facing the visitor as he crosses the bridge over the dry moat is dated 1598. The hall, which has a flat ceiling, contains a large and curious Elizabethan chimney-piece at the lower end, while the wall and canopy above the dais at the other end are lined with imported Flemish panelling, containing carved reliefs, of about 1530. The parlour has a very rich Elizabethan ceiling modelled with sprays of roses, and a curious carved relief representing all the Norris family in about 1565. The property was sold in 1794 to Mr Richard Watt, who carefully preserved the ancient house, his descendant Miss Adelaide Watt bequeathing it to descendants of the original Norris owners. From them it was received in 1944 by the National Trust, and is now leased to the Corporation of Liverpool as an historical museum.

64. IN THE TUDOR HALL

65. LITTLE MORETON HALL: THE GABLES OF THE HALL PORCH AND BAY WINDOWS, 1559

Little Moreton Hall, Astbury, Cheshire. (The National Trust.) Most picturesque of the black-and-white houses of Cheshire and Lancashire, Little Moreton Hall owes its curious appearance to three generations of the Moreton family. It consists of a long and lofty gatehouse range, overlooking the moat, and providing a self-contained dwelling in itself; and, behind it, the mansion-house proper forming the second and third sides of the courtyard. The hall belonged originally to the Rufford-Adlington type, with Gothic roof and 'speres', probably built *c.* 1520, which is perhaps the date of the two lower storeys of the gatehouse also. In 1559, William Moreton added to the hall a sumptuous porch and bay window, with another to the parlour at right angles, in such a way that their projecting upper storeys meet together. They bear the inscription that 'Richard Dale, Carpenter, made these windows by the grace of God', and the date. They then felt a need for a fashionable long gallery, and decided that the only place for it was above the gatehouse range. Accordingly, a fantastic upper storey was added to this about 1580, its sides consisting entirely of elaborately leaded windows. Its roof-structure followed the Gothic pattern, but the end-gables were decorated with painted plaster reliefs. The other rooms contain massively wrought woodwork and chimney-pieces. Though long occupied as a farm-house, later Moretons continued to maintain the historic old building, which descended to the late Bishop Abraham, its donor to the Trust. A descendant, or namesake, of Carpenter Dale has been for many years the caretaker.

66. THE GALLERY AT THE TOP OF THE GATEHOUSE, 1580

67. LITTLE MORETON HALL: MOST PICTURESQUE OF BLACK-AND-WHITE CHESHIRE HOUSES

68. CHARLECOTE: THE APPROACH BENEATH SIR THOMAS LUCY'S GATEHOUSE

Charlecote Park, Stratford-on-Avon, Warwickshire. (The National Trust; *Sir M. Fairfax-Lucy*.) Sir Thomas Lucy, in 1558, rebuilt the house in which his ancestors had lived since 1189 beside the River Avon. Traditionally it was in the deer park that the young Shakespeare was arrested when poaching, and was punished by Sir Thomas—later satirized in the character of Justice Shallow. The house, containing many portraits (16th–18th centuries), has been altered from time to time.

69. CHRISTCHURCH MANSION

Christchurch Mansion, Ipswich, Suffolk. (Ipswich Corporation.) Now maintained as an Art Gallery and Museum of domestic antiquities and period furniture, the house was built in 1550 by Edmund Withipole, of a line of London and Bristol merchants. It became the home of the French Huguenot family of Fonnereau in 1732 till 1892, when it was saved from demolition by Mr F. T. Cobbold, who presented it to Ipswich with (in 1909) an endowment fund for its present use. Most of the interior was burnt in 1675, when it was richly redecorated in the late Stuart style. The collection, including much furniture of this and the Tudor period, also contains important paintings of the East Anglian school.

Harvington Hall, Kidderminster, Worcestershire. (The Roman Catholic Archdiocese of Birmingham.) This picturesque moated manor house, built between 1569–78 by John Pakington, has been untouched structurally since about 1700. It is remarkable for the large number of secret hiding-places, ingeniously contrived at or soon after the time of building, for the use of its Catholic owners and their priests.[1] There are also very notable remains of the mural decorations executed about 1577.

[1] Other houses (not illustrated) with well-preserved hiding-places, which were used by Charles II after the Battle of Worcester, are Mosely Old Hall and Boscobel House, both near Wolverhampton.

70. HARVINGTON HALL

71. LOSELEY PARK: THE FRONT, BUILT 1561-69

Loseley Park, Guildford, Surrey. (Mr J. R. More-Molyneux.) The builder of Loseley, where a house existed from much earlier times, was Sir William More, a kinsman of the Blessed Sir Thomas More, and son of Sir Christopher More, a trusted servant of Henry VIII. Building accounts show the work to have occupied the years 1561-69, so that the house is one of the earliest built under Queen Elizabeth—who often visited Loseley. The design is an interesting development from Gothic tradition towards the stricter symmetry and more restrained lines of the next age. A plan by the Jacobean surveyor John Thorpe shows a gatehouse like that of Charlecote, and two wings enclosing a forecourt. One wing was certainly built, in 1600, but was pulled down in 1830. The materials consist of ragstone from the ruins of Waverley Abbey near Farnham, and the local hard chalk—in which is carved a number of ornate chimney-pieces in the house. The hall preserves its original form, but has been frequently altered. Its most interesting feature is a series of carved, inlaid, and painted panels brought in 1685 from Henry VIII's fantastic palace of Nonsuch. Other rooms contain elaborate ceilings, *c.* 1600, and good 17th- and 18th-century family portraits. The late 17th-century terrace gardens, laid out in the moat of the earlier house, are picturesque.

72. THE HALL, WITH HENRY VIII PANELLING FROM NONSUCH PALACE

73. PARHAM: THE SOUTH FRONT TOWARDS THE DOWNS, 1577

Parham Park, Pulborough, Sussex. (The Hon. Clive Pearson.) Beautifully placed facing the Sussex Downs in an ancient deer park, the building of Parham was begun in 1577 by Sir Thomas Palmer, of a Sussex family of mercers, on land belonging till the Dissolution to Westminster Abbey. In 1601, Thomas Palmer, who had held naval commands under Drake and Hawkins, sold the property to Sir Thomas Bishop, 1st baronet, whose wife was a Weston of Sutton Place (p. 53). His descendants, who inherited the ancient peerage of Zouche, continued in possession till 1922, when Mr Pearson bought it with all its contents and undertook extensive repairs.

The design closely resembles that of Loseley. Alterations in 1710 and 1790 have contributed to the interest of the interior without spoiling the principal feature—the beautiful great hall. This is lit by lofty many-mullioned windows, and retains its original plaster ceiling, above which runs a long gallery. The remarkable and continuous series of Bishop family portraits (1600–1870) has been supplemented by Mr Pearson with an outstanding group of Elizabethan and Jacobean historic portraits. The rooms, ranging in date from Elizabethan to Adam, contain period furnishings of no less quality.

74. THE GREAT HALL, HUNG WITH ELIZABETHAN PORTRAITS

75. HOGHTON TOWER: THE INNER COURT

Hoghton Tower, Preston, Lancashire. (Sir Cuthbert de Hoghton, Bt.) Hoghtons were living in 'the house on the hill', as the name means, in the 12th century. Serving as mayors of Preston or sheriffs of the county, they lived conservatively, keeping up old customs. When James I came to Hoghton in 1617 to hunt in its once-famous park, Sir Richard Hoghton persuaded all the neighbouring gentry to don his livery for the occasion. His father had rebuilt the mansion (1565) in the old fashion that had prevailed a century earlier. So Hoghton Tower on its hill, though now almost surrounded by modern industry, is a Lancashire Haddon Hall. The gateway beneath the battlemented tower gives into the outer court, which is divided by another, wrought-iron, gate, whence a paved way contained by balustrades leads up to the inner gateway and to the inner court containing a statue of William III and the hall range. In 1710 the family moved elsewhere, and Hoghton was not lived in by them again until the end of the 19th century, when Sir Henry de Hoghton and his son restored their old home with admirable care. Besides the stone-walled, oak-roofed hall itself, containing furniture of its period and relics of King James's visit, there are panelled rooms of the late 17th century and pictures of local interest.

76. THE GATEHOUSE

77. ROCKINGHAM CASTLE: ELIZABETHAN PEEPING OVER MEDIEVAL RAMPARTS

Rockingham Castle, Market Harborough, Northamptonshire. (Commander Sir M. Culme-Seymour, Bt.) A hunting palace of Plantagenet kings in Rockingham Forest, of which the 12th-century outer walls remain, the castle was granted to Edward Watson, ancestor of the present owner, in 1554. The picturesque medley of buildings within were erected at various times from the 13th to the 19th centuries, but the Elizabethan predominate, with some attractive work of the Charles II period. A long gallery contains portraits of interest, and Rockingham Church fine monuments to the Earls of Rockingham.

St Fagan's Castle, Cardiff. (The National Museum of Wales.) The gabled Elizabethan manor house built about 1570 is likewise surrounded by the battlemented walls of a Welsh border castle, set on high ground overlooking a still rural valley. From the Welsh family of Lewis it passed by marriage about 1700 to the 3rd Earl of Plymouth, whose descendant, the late Earl, gave the castle to the National Museum of Wales. Gardens of much charm were made among the ramparts and old fishponds by Lady Windsor in the 19th century, which are now the setting for the newly formed Welsh National Folk Museum.

78. ST FAGAN'S CASTLE

79. LEVENS HALL: THE ELIZABETHAN HOUSE (1586), INCORPORATING A TOWER OF 1350

80. THE TOPIARY GARDEN, PLANTED ABOUT 1700

81. LEVENS HALL: ELIZABETHAN PLASTERWORK IN THE HALL

Levens Hall, Kendal, Westmorland. (Mr O. R. Bagot.) Sir James Bellingham, who reigned at Levens from 1577 till 1641, as a young man converted a medieval stronghold into the smiling Elizabethan country house which remains little altered. Till then it consisted, like Sizergh (p. 33), in a pele-tower dating from 1350 with a great hall attached, which had been the home of the Redeman family till 1489. Sir James, who put the date 1586 on his work, used many of the old walls, but set his hall at first-floor level, reached by a flight of steps against the tower that he also built. Above the wainscot, its ceiling and walls are adorned with enriched plasterwork, introducing painted shields of Bellingham heraldry and all kinds of strange animals. The adjoining drawing-rooms have similar ceilings and enriched wainscot, with elaborate overmantels in the same style as those at Sizergh. That of the smaller drawing-room, representing the Elements, Seasons, and Senses, is probably imported North German work.

About 1687, Alan Bellingham had gambled away his estate to Colonel James Grahme, a son of the warlike Border Grahmes of Netherby and a court official of James II, whose private affairs he continued to superintend even after the King's flight. Colonel Grahme did little to the house, but a great deal outside, bringing into existence the extraordinary garden—the most perfect and extensive example surviving of the topiary style of about 1700. The designer is recorded to have been Monsieur Beaumont, gardener to King James II at Hampton Court, and reputedly a pupil of Le Nôtre. It consists of walled enclosures laid out in geometrical beds, no doubt intended for the then fashionable tulips and pinks, interspersed with great numbers of yew trees, grotesquely clipped into the shapes of mushrooms, umbrellas, chessmen, and arches; or into continuous hedged alleys. Particularly beautiful are the clipped beech hedges, 250 years old.

82. HALL-I'-THE-WOOD, BOLTON: WHERE TUDOR AND JACOBEAN MEET

Hall-i'-the-Wood, Bolton, Lancashire. (The Corporation of Bolton.) Industry has long replaced the woods among which the timbered hall of the Brownlowe family was built about 1590 on the hills overlooking Bolton. In 1648, when a Norris of Speke (p. 55) inherited it by marriage, he added to his wife's home a stone building of no less size and pretension. And so the two, representing two different epochs, have stood ever since. The late Lord Leverhulme restored the house and presented it as a museum to the town.

Bramhall Hall, Stockport, Lancashire. (Hazel Grove and Bramhall Urban District Council.) Another example, from the Cheshire-Lancashire borders, of how the Tudor gentry of those parts housed themselves. The Davenport family became established at Bramhall about 1400, but not till 1590, it is recorded, did Sir William and Dame Dorothy Davenport build the present house round a courtyard. The many-gabled oriel windows of the hall resemble the work of Carpenter Dale at Little Moreton (p. 56). The old house was bought and thoroughly restored by the late C. H. Nevill at the end of last century, with William Devey as his architect. It is now used as a museum.

83. BRAMHALL HALL: THE ENTRANCE

VI. Elizabethan Renaissance, 1550–1600

THE traditional techniques, enlivened with Italian titbits, and labelled 'Tudor' in these notes, continued throughout the 16th century. But in its middle years the more cultivated of the new men enriched by the Tudor revolution promoted an authentic English version of the European 'Renaissance' style, derived from some study of classical architecture. The new architecture's development was shaped, however, by the vagaries of Tudor foreign and religious policy, which barred contact with Rome after 1558, maintained varying relations with France, and tended to ever closer ties with the Protestant Netherlands and German states.

The consequence was that the direct influence exerted by Italy in the early stages of the English Renaissance was of too short duration to produce a distinct classical architecture; French models predominated between 1550–70; and thenceforward the Flemish mannerism (usually termed Jacobean)

prevailed 1580–1625. Individual designers, surveyors, and master-masons, though scarcely yet possessing the status of architects, begin to be distinguishable.

Through the medium of these foreign idioms the zestful spirit of the Elizabethan Age—adventurous, romantic, ostentatious, and scholarly—expresses itself in original beauty. But it was by no means only classical in intention. In seeking a substitute for outmoded Gothic tradition, the Elizabethans drew upon perennial springs of 'romance', which were to fertilize architecture no less in succeeding centuries. Such buildings as Wollaton Hall, Hardwick Hall, and Bolsover Castle reflect the same psychology as Spenser's *Faerie Queene*, and a scale of values, an attitude to life, which sought to perpetuate in towers and battlements and stately halls the spirit of medieval chivalry and traditions of the almost vanished feudal order. In that sense their design was consciously picturesque.

84. LONGLEAT, BUILT 1540–80: THE FIRST GREAT HOUSE OF THE ENGLISH RENAISSANCE

Longleat, Warminster, Wiltshire. (The Marquess of Bath.) Longleat, begun in 1541 and not completed till after 1580, occupies a unique place among the origins of English Renaissance architecture, illustrating the high-water mark attained by the French influence. Its builder, Sir John Thynne, was a close associate of Protector Somerset, William Cecil the statesman and builder of Burleigh House, Stamford, Sir Thomas Gresham, the founder of the Royal Exchange, and Sir W. Sharington of Lacock (p. 28), who were all amateurs of the new architecture. He employed a succession of designers, but was himself the directing intelligence behind the gradual transformation of a

ruinous priory into a palace of outstanding originality. Its fronts are strictly symmetrical, with ranges of immense windows looking outward (instead of to inner courts); the roof is flat instead of ridged and gabled, and is surmounted by domed pavilions (as in some French prototypes); and the tiers of classical orders are accurately applied. The majestic pile is situated in an 18th-century park of exceptional beauty.

Most of the interior, containing notable paintings, was redecorated in the Italian style about 1860. But a traditional great hall which was incorporated remains little altered, and is hung with large hunting scenes by Wootton (1730).

85. KIRBY HALL: THE RUINED PORCH DATED 1575

Kirby Hall, near Kettering, Northants. (The Ministry of Works.) Begun in 1570, the design of hall and porch is French in inspiration, and was probably due to the same group of amateurs who devised Longleat and Burleigh, the mason being John Thorpe senior. Inigo Jones made additions to the house about 1640.

86. WOLLATON HALL, AN ELIZABETHAN CASTLE

Wollaton Hall, Nottingham. (The Corporation of Nottingham.) Built 1580–85 for Sir Francis Willoughby. The architect, Robert Smithson, had worked on Longleat, with which Wollaton has many points of design in common: its outward-facing ranges of huge windows, its flat roof with elaborated corner pavilions, and classical orders. But the restraint and somewhat French refinement of Longleat has given place to the over-richness and over-emphasis of the Flemish mannerism. The traditional character of the hall is similar to Longleat, but here it is placed in the centre of the plan, and its roof is carried up to form a dominating tower-like mass, giving a castellated effect to the whole. It illustrates the romantic strain in the Elizabethans.

The family of the Willoughbys had possessed Wollaton since the 14th century, and the builder's great-uncle was Sir Hugh Willoughby, the navigator who discovered Nova Zembla. Sir Francis derived his wealth from industrial and commercial interests, a fact which may help to account for the opulence and affected medievalism of his mansion—so curiously akin to that of a Victorian captain of industry.

The interior of Wollaton contains later decorations in the manner of Verrio, and is now used as the city's natural history museum.

87. THE ROOF OF THE GREAT HALL

**88. COBHAM HALL: THE WEST ELE-
VATION, 1580–1667**

Cobham Hall, Cobham, Kent. (The Earl of
Darnley.) Much of England's history has moved
along the road from London to Canterbury and
Dover past Cobham, but the medieval Lords
Cobham lived at Cooling Castle, and the Hall was
not begun till 1580 by the 10th Lord. Building was
interrupted by the threat of Spanish invasion in
1588, and was not finished when Queen Elizabeth
died. The central block was rebuilt in 1667 for the
5th Duke of Lennox, created Lord Cobham by
Charles II. The wings, however, ending in turrets,
and the disposition about a court, are typical of
late Tudor design. What gives them their Elizabethan character are the Flemish-classical porches
of the wings dated 1594, executed by a certain
Giles de Witt. This artist probably also worked the
elaborate marble chimney-pieces in the house.
The centre block was rebuilt in 1662 and contains
the magnificent Golden Hall. Cobham Hall passed
by marriage in 1713 to the Earl of Darnley, whose
successors subsequently employed James Wyatt
and Humphry Repton on the Hall and stately park.

**89. THE PORCH OF THE NORTH WING,
DESIGNED BY GILES DE WITT**

90. MONTACUTE: THE EAST FRONT, 1599

Montacute, Yeovil, Somerset. (The National Trust.) Elizabethan architecture achieved one of its masterpieces in this beautiful building, erected for Sir Edward Phelips, a West Country lawyer, in 1595. Its designer is unknown; but the masons were probably descendants of those of Ham Hill who built Barrington (p. 54), seventy-five years earlier, of the same golden stone. The richness contributed by the exquisite forecourt pavilions and balustrades, the roof outline, the great areas of glass, and the sculptured figures in niches, is balanced by the firm, clean, wall surfaces. The 'H' plan, with staircases in the angles of the west side, is no less the perfected outcome of Tudor usage. The interior, retaining much contemporary decoration, now contains a very fine collection of furniture and pictures formed by the National Trust, to which the house was transferred soon after the tenure of the Phelips family ended.

Since 1786, the entrance has been in the west front through the porch, then brought from Clifton Maybank, Dorsetshire. This exquisite example of the earlier phase of Renaissance design, under Franco-Italian influence, was built for Sir Edward Horsey about 1546.

91. ONE SIDE OF THE FORECOURT AND A GARDEN PAVILION

92. MONTACUTE: THE WEST ENTRANCE, *c.* 1546

93. HARDWICK HALL, 1590: THE CLIMAX OF ELIZABETHAN RENAISSANCE DESIGN

Hardwick Hall, Chesterfield, Derbyshire. (The Chatsworth Estate Company ; *The Duchess of Devonshire.*) Built by 'Bess of Hardwick' (1522–1607)—successively Elizabeth Hardwick, Mrs Barlow, Lady Cavendish, Lady St. Loe, and Countess of Shrewsbury—during her last widowhood after 1590. This remarkable lady, whose career began at the court of Henry VIII and Anne Boleyn, and ended under James I, is among the most vivid characters of the Elizabethan Renaissance, the arts of which she carried to their climax in this lovely building and its precious contents. It is the second house which she built here: the ruins of the first, in which Mary Queen of Scots is traditionally said to have been detained, stand adjacent; and she also built the first great house of Chatsworth. Her ambition was only matched by her zest for building superbly, and her building by her zest for needlework.

Robert Smithson, who worked at Longleat and built Wollaton, may have had a hand in the design of Hardwick, which has affinities with both. But Bess's own individuality is writ as large in its peculiarities as are her initials on the tops of its towers.

The design is the product of a passion for light—displayed in the innumerable and vast windows ('Hardwick Hall, more glass than wall', the old jingle goes)—and of her placing the principal rooms on the top storey. The hall runs from back to front in the middle, a gallery the whole length of the upper storey at the back, and at that level the front is occupied by 'the High Great Presence Chamber'. A frieze in clear-coloured relief of forest scenes, spring and summer, the court of Diana, and the story of Orpheus, runs round the walls of this room which, with its contemporary furniture and faded tapestries, has been described by Mr Sitwell as 'the most beautiful in the whole of Europe'. It may well be the most romantic, approached as it is by a vast stone staircase which climbs through half the building's length.

Every room holds beauty, in sculptured alabaster or moulded plaster chimney-pieces, elaborate wainscot, painted or woven hangings. Through them all, like a refrain, runs the motto, to which the key is lost:

The redolent smell of eglantine
We stagges exalt to the Divine.

94. HARDWICK HALL: THE HIGH GREAT PRESENCE CHAMBER

Much of the abounding needlework has been attributed to Mary Queen of Scots, during her long detention at Chatsworth, and some small pieces are undoubtedly her work. The famous set of velvet hangings in the hall, embroidered with the Virtues and traditionally worked by the Queen, may have been made by French needlewomen for her apartments at Chatsworth.

Throughout the house the floors are of plaster, covered with rush matting.

Hardwick Hall, on Lady Shrewsbury's death, passed to her Cavendish descendants, and has been preserved intact by successive Dukes of Devonshire. Among innumerable portraits is one of Thomas Hobbes, the philosopher, tutor to the Cavendish boys.

95. HARDWICK HALL: THE STAIRCASE

96. EMBROIDERED VELVET HANGINGS, 'THE VIRTUES', 1575, IN THE HALL AT HARDWICK

97. BURTON AGNES HALL: THE GATEHOUSE

Burton Agnes, Driffield, Yorkshire. (Mr Marcus Wickham-Boynton.) A London architect must have conceived this very remarkable house built by Sir Henry Griffith in 1600–10, for it has little in common with other Yorkshire houses, but is one of the most mature of late Elizabethan designs. Approached through a gatehouse with four domed turrets, the front is a symmetrical composition contained by gabled wings with bow windows, between which project turrets, one containing the porch. Within, the decoration is lavish.

The Elizabethan staircase has no less than eight newels, coupled into pairs with arches and their surfaces covered with carving, which, with the balustrades, build up a composition of extraordinary intricacy. The hall screen, itself elaborately carved (p. 78), is surmounted by three tiers of allegorical plaster reliefs of exceptional interest. The chimney-piece (*c.* 1588), similarly adorned with the parable of the Wise and Foolish Virgins, was brought from Barmston Hall by Sir Griffith Boynton in 1760 when the hall ceiling was inserted. Above it was a great gallery with a richly modelled barrel-vault ceiling similar to that of Chastleton (p. 79), which unfortunately collapsed in the 19th century. Other rooms retain their full contemporary decoration.

98. THE PORCH IN THE MAIN FRONT

99. BURTON AGNES: THE STAIRCASE

100. BURTON AGNES: THE HALL

101. CHASTLETON HOUSE: THE LONG GALLERY

102. CHASTLETON HOUSE, 1603–12: THE ENTRANCE FRONT

Chastleton House, near Moreton-in-Marsh, Oxfordshire. (Mrs Whitmore-Jones.) The most perfectly preserved of early 17th-century manor houses, retaining contemporary furnishings of exceptional interest. Though begun in the first year of James I's reign, Chastleton represents the final development of the medium-sized Elizabethan house from such earlier types as Loseley (p. 60), Parham (p. 61) and Levens Hall (p. 65). The estate was bought in 1602 from Robert Catesby (subsequently beheaded for his part in the 'Gunpowder Plot') by Walter Jones, a prosperous Witney clothier. The house he built, 1603–12, closely resembles Burton Agnes in plan and arrangement, though smaller, and is approached by a gateway similar to Charlton House (p. 90). Staircases of continuous newels are contained in the two towers at either end; the entrance is by the left of the two projections on the front. The hall retains its screen and wainscot complete, and most of the rooms, which lie round a small court, have enriched ceilings, fireplaces, and wainscot. The long gallery (p. 79), at the top of the house above the hall as at Burton Agnes and Montacute, is in this case complete with its barrel-vaulted ceiling patterned with roses and its untouched silvery oak wainscot. The furnishing of the Witney's clothier's house is detailed in an inventory of 1633, and much of it is still *in situ*, besides historical and personal relics of the Civil War period. After the Battle of Worcester (1651), Arthur Jones was saved from Cromwellian pursuers by his wife's heroism and an effective secret hiding-place.

103. KELMSCOTT: WILLIAM MORRIS'S MANOR HOUSE

Kelmscott Manor, Lechlade, Oxfordshire. (The University of Oxford.) In 1871 William Morris fell in love with, and acquired, the grey gabled manor house lying among the Thames-side water-meadows and enclosed in a romantic old garden. It was probably built about 1570, in the style traditional of the Cotswolds, on the fringe of which it stands. But Morris's coming is the more significant date; for it converted him, and directed the artistic revival, in the England which he represented, to the sensitive restoration of old buildings and away from the creation of a modern idiom. Whether that was a good thing or not, his tender, self-effacing care inspired two generations to preserve ancient buildings, and made of Kelmscott an exquisitely beautiful place. (The house, privately inhabited, is open by appointment on Wednesdays and Saturdays to those especially interested in Morris's work.)

Fountains Hall, near Ripon, Yorkshire (The Studley Estate Company), was built adjoining, and from the stones of, the great Yorkshire Abbey of Fountains, by Sir Stephen Proctor, about 1600. He had bought the Abbey from Sir Richard Gresham, a prominent London business-man, its purchaser at the Dissolution. In design it is a miniature Montacute, with close affinities to Chastleton and the façade of Sir Paul Pindar's house in Bishopsgate (built 1600, now in the Victoria and Albert Museum), adapted to its site against the steep side of a valley. These associations suggest that the designer of this extremely accomplished little building was a Londoner.

104. FOUNTAINS HALL

105. KNOLE, FROM THE GARDEN

JACOBEAN England enjoyed the splendour inherited from the Elizabethan age but without quite its youth and zest. One of King James's first acts was to end the long and latterly unsuccessful war with Spain which had impoverished the country during the last twenty years of the great Queen. The wealth and energy released thereby, and the emulation attending the growth of a new aristocracy in place of that destroyed by the early Tudors, encouraged the outburst in the arts which, though generated under Elizabeth and usually associated with her reign, reached its full extent and maturity under James—notwithstanding the growing sectarian and political cleavage represented by Puritanism which was to rend the kingdom under his son.

At first sight, Jacobean architecture is continuous and identical with Elizabethan, just as Shakespeare's later plays fulfilled the promise of those written before 1603, and as Robert Cecil, Earl of Salisbury, the principal Minister, carried on the administrative efficiency of his father, Lord Burghley, the Queen's great Secretary. There is, however, a marked distinction. A number of great houses came into existence which differ from those created during the previous generation by their sheer size, and by their emphasis on 'state' in place of the Elizabethans' originality or homeliness. This stateliness is reflected in the increasingly symmetrical planning, although the elevations continued to present picturesque variety of outline. The ornamentation, derived predominantly from Flemish patterns, is no less lavish than

[*continued, p. 84*

106. THE HALL, IN STONE COURT

107. KNOLE: THE GREAT STAIRCASE

108. KNOLE: THE LEICESTER GALLERY

previously, but tends to repeat conventional patterns, of which the effect is curious intricacy.

Then in 1617 the building of the Queen's House, Greenwich, and in 1619 of the Banqueting House, Whitehall, by Inigo Jones in the authentic classical style of Palladio, introduced a new era in English architecture. Had not the political situation begun to deteriorate, Italian classicism would have been well established in England by 1650, instead of delayed for another seventy years, first by the reactionary Puritan régime of the Commonwealth, and subsequently by the magnificent vernacular achievement of Wren and his school.

Knole, Sevenoaks, Kent. (The National Trust; *Lord Sackville.*) Knole, perhaps the most famous and representative of all English country houses, illustrates incomparably the first Jacobean decade. Originally a palace of the medieval Archbishops of Canterbury and lying in a noble park, the rambling mansion was transformed internally by Thomas Sackville, 1st Earl of Dorset. Its beauty lies less in the relatively small rooms and galleries in which it consists than in its unparalleled wealth of decoration and historic and artistic contents, much of it dating from 1610, but continuously supplemented during the later 17th and the 18th centuries. In these the texture and mellow colouring of plasterwork, brocade, gilding, and tapestry, veneered and silver furniture, and a superb range of portraits, compose a whole that is as unforgettable as it is indescribable.

109. CHIMNEY-PIECE OF INLAID MARBLES IN THE BALLROOM

110. AUDLEY END: THE FRONT FROM ACROSS THE RIVER CAM

Audley End, Saffron Walden, Essex. (The Ministry of Works.) Impressive as is the many-turreted and windowed stone front seen today, only a third survives of the 'palace', built, probably under his own supervision, by Thomas Howard, 1st Earl of Suffolk, 1603–16. Originally, a great outer court, with tall angle pavilions, stretched forward halfway to the river, and an inner courtyard lay behind the existing hall range. The two two-storeyed porches at either end of the hall are massively 'classical', and may have convinced the Earl that he was building in the true Roman style, but the pinnacled turrets, many-mullioned windows, and the importance accorded to the hall reflect Tudor tradition. Lying, as Audley End does, on the road to Newmarket, and far too large as it became for later needs, the 3rd Earl succeeded in selling it to Charles II as a country palace. William III returned it to the 5th Earl, who, advised by Vanbrugh, in 1721 pulled down two-thirds of the building. Vanbrugh redecorated one end of the hall also, but the extremely ornate and characteristic Jacobean screen is unaltered. About 1776 the principal living-rooms were redecorated by Biagio Rebecca in the Adam and a version of the Jacobean styles; others are of 1834. In 1762 the property descended to the 1st Lord Braybrooke, whose grandson earned posterity's gratitude by first deciphering and giving to the world Pepys's *Diary*. Audley End was acquired by the State from his descendant.

111. THE HALL ORIEL AND PORCH

112. AUDLEY END: THE HALL SCREEN

113. HATFIELD HOUSE: THE HALL

114. HATFIELD HOUSE: THE ENTRANCE FRONT

Hatfield House, Hertfordshire. (The Marquess of Salisbury.) Adjoining the mansion built 1607–12 by Robert Cecil, 1st Earl of Salisbury, is Hatfield Old Palace, where Queen Elizabeth was confined during her sister Mary's reign. The Bishops of Ely's palace prior to acquisition by the Crown, James I exchanged it for Theobalds House with his Minister. The accounts for the present building show that the design is due to Robert Lyminge (*d.* 1628), supervised by Simon Basil, predecessor of Inigo Jones as Surveyor of the King's Works. Despite the building's great size, the façades of mellow brick and stone are domestic, as contrasted with palatial (as at Audley End), in scale, and the plan is among the earliest to combine domestic comfort with provision for 'state'. The whole centre is devoted to the State Rooms, which, although including the traditional great hall (p. 87), made an innovation by also providing a separate dining-room with kitchen adjacent. Convenient communications are provided by the long gallery's becoming the main upper corridor, while the staircase, exquisitely designed and decorated, is spaciously planned. The family living quarters consist of relatively modest rooms contained in the wings. Though somewhat redecorated in 1878 (e.g. the Hall), Hatfield House is one of the most completely adorned and preserved of the great Jacobean mansions, and contains an unsurpassed collection of 16th- and 17th-century historical portraits, also of the statesmen so consistently produced by the Cecil family.

115. THE STAIRCASE

116. BLICKLING HALL: THE APPROACH

Blickling Hall, Aylsham, Norfolk. (The National Trust; *Mr Somerset de Chair*.) In its beautiful setting of lawns and gardens, the rose-red brick mansion of Blickling, many-gabled and tur-reted, satisfies the most romantic conception of the English country house. It was built 1616–28, on the moated site of a house previously belonging to the Boleyn family, for Sir Henry Hobart from designs by Robert Lyminge, architect of Hatfield House with which it has much in common. The curved and pedi-mented gables are a Dutch feature characteristic of this date and especially of East Anglia. The grand staircase is a close counter-part to that at Hatfield and probably by the same carver, but assumed its present arrangement and position in the 18th cen-tury, when it was re-erected in the former great hall. The long gallery has a particularly elaborate plaster ceiling modelled with emblematical devices. Some of the principal rooms, including the hall, were decorated, *c.* 1770, by the Norwich architect William Ivory for the Earl of Buckinghamshire. They contain notable Chinese wall-papers and St Petersburg tapestry (given by the Empress Catherine). Blickling descended to the late Marquess of Lothian, ambassador and statesman, who not only gave the property to the National Trust, but originated the extension of the Trust's activities to the holding of historic houses.

117. THE STAIRCASE

118. CHARLTON HOUSE

Charlton House, Greenwich (London). (Greenwich Borough Council.) Built by Sir Adam Newton, Secretary to Henry, Prince of Wales, eldest son of James I, in 1607–12. Charlton may be compared with Ham House (p. 103), as it was before alteration, which was the suburban home of another Court official of the period. Charlton has a fine staircase, moulded ceilings, and grotesquely modelled chimney-pieces, the designs for some of which were printed by Abraham de Bruyn.

119. TEMPLE NEWSAM: THE GARDEN SIDE

120. THE LONG GALLERY

Temple Newsam, Leeds, Yorkshire. (The Corporation of Leeds.) Lord Darnley, afterwards husband of Mary, Queen of Scots, was born at Temple Newsam—so called from having originally been a preceptory of the Knights Templar. The oldest part dates from *c.* 1550, but the house was virtually rebuilt in 1630 by Sir Arthur Ingram. The dignity of the design, simplified from the ornate exuberance of Jacobean buildings, represents the taste of Charles I's early years. In the 18th century the 7th Viscount Irwin redecorated much of the interior, employing the York school of craftsmen. In 1922, the Hon. Edward Wood (Lord Irwin and present Earl of Halifax) sold the property to the Leeds Corporation. The Hall is now the city's principal art gallery, containing important permanent and loan collections of furniture and pictures.

121. ASTON HALL: THE FORECOURT

Aston Hall, Birmingham. (The Corporation of Birmingham.)
Sir Thomas Holte, who built Aston Hall 1618–35, came of an
old family of Warwickshire gentry having no particular connection with Birmingham, then a market town beginning to be
noted for its smiths. Charles I was Sir Thomas's guest before
the Battle of Edgehill at the beginning of the Civil War. The
design of the building follows the general pattern set by Hatfield
and Blickling, with turrets and curved gables, but includes
original features, such as the balustraded central portion containing the hall. The massive carved oak staircase and the long
gallery are particularly fine, and there are typical decorated
ceilings and chimney-pieces. The Holte family continued to
flourish till the end of the 18th century. In 1857, when there was
danger of the house being demolished, a private company was
formed to acquire the mansion and gardens for public use. They
were subsequently vested in the Corporation of Birmingham,
affording one of the first instances of civic enterprise on these
lines. Aston Hall is now the City of Birmingham Museum and
Art Gallery and, besides its original features, contains an
exhibition of period rooms. In these the development of interior
decoration from Tudor to Victorian times, and of the accompanying techniques of furniture design, needlework, textiles,
pottery, metal-work, etc., is illustrated by examples collected
from the vicinity.

122. THE LONG GALLERY

123.   BOLSOVER CASTLE ON ITS HIGH RIDGE

Bolsover Castle, Chesterfield, Derbyshire. (The Ministry of Works.) Peveril of the Peak had a stronghold on this rock in the 12th century, but all we now see is Jacobean—an astonishing example of the conservatism, or 'romanticism', of Shakespeare's contemporaries displayed also at Wollaton (p. 69) and Hardwick (p. 73). Sir Charles Cavendish, its builder, was a son of Bess of Hardwick, and his architect was John Smithson, a relation of the architect of Wollaton. The conception of the keep was consciously medieval, and its construction is in the real Gothic tradition. But all the decoration, which was of utmost splendour, is elaborately Renaissance in style. Several rooms have remarkable painted decoration, and the sculptured chimney-pieces of alabaster and marble are unique. Adjoining the keep is the enormous shell of a more classical range added by that great Royalist horseman, the Cavendish Duke of Newcastle, who entertained Charles I in it at immense expense in 1634. His Riding School is nearly as palatial, and there are remains of the remarkable contemporary garden. The ducal inheritance passed later to the Harley and so to the Bentinck family. The castle was ceded to the State for maintenance by the present Duke of Portland.

124.   THE VAULTED HALL OF BOLSOVER

125. CASTLE ASHBY: THE GARDEN FRONT, 1624

Castle Ashby, Northampton. (The Marquess of Northampton.) Approached by splendid avenues of *c.* 1700, and lying in a great landscape park by Capability Brown (1765), the present quadrangular mansion takes the place of a castle crenellated in 1306. Henry, grandson of Sir William Compton, of Compton Wynyates (p. 48), began building it *c.* 1575, when he was created Lord Compton; but the bulk is regional Jacobean of 1624, due to his son, the 1st Earl of Northampton. The traditional façades present the most complete example of a balustrade spelling out an inscription (*see* Hardwick, p. 73), in this case the verse *Nisi Dominus.* . . . About 1630, however, the fourth side, containing the entrance to the courtyard, was completed in the new classical manner, with little doubt by Inigo Jones. The interior presents work of many dates up to 1883, but predominantly of the Charles I period. The Great Chamber, with Elizabethan and Charles II features, has a ceiling of *c.* 1624, when others were also set up. Its plasterwork typifies the transition in style from the Jacobean (e.g. Aston Hall, p. 92) to the Palladian (cf. Wilton, p. 96). A richly carved oak staircase and a room of exceptional painted panelling are also of this epoch. The State Rooms, hung with Brussels and other tapestries, were decorated *c.* 1675 by the 3rd Earl to repair Civil War damage, and contain excellent furniture of that period.

**126. THE INIGO JONES SIDE OF THE COURT-
YARD**

127. CASTLE ASHBY: THE GREAT CHAMBER, c. 1624

128. WILTON HOUSE: THE INIGO JONES FRONT, 1647

Wilton House, Salisbury, Wiltshire. (The Earl of Pembroke.) Since 1541, when Henry VIII gave the former abbey to Sir William Herbert, 1st Earl of Pembroke, army commander and politician in three reigns, Wilton House has been the home of a family noted in the arts. Of the first building, designed in 1543 by Holbein, only the porch (now a garden house) and the courtyard plan survive. The 2nd Earl and his Countess, Mary Sidney, Sir Philip's sister (see Penshurst, p. 40), had made it 'like a college, so many were the learned and ingenious persons' assembled. *As You Like It* was first performed at Wilton. William, 3rd Earl, and Philip, 4th Earl—'the incomparable pair of brethren' to whom Shakespeare dedicated the first Folio of his plays—transformed it,

first to match the celebrated formal gardens laid out (1633) by de Caux, and then to make good a disastrous fire in 1647. At this date the 4th Earl, who had favoured the Parliamentary cause, engaged Inigo Jones to design the new south front. His work at Wilton was his outstanding performance among private houses. The 9th Earl, with Roger Morris, designed (1737) the Palladian Bridge facing Jones's front, when William Kent was replacing the old formal gardens with cedar-shaded lawns and spacious landscapes, to which Sir William Chambers added later embellishments. But what survived of the original building suffered when the 11th Earl employed James Wyatt in his Gothic phase to rebuild the north and west fronts, including the great hall.

129. WILTON HOUSE: THE DOUBLE CUBE ROOM, c. 1650, DESIGNED BY INIGO JONES; THE PORTRAITS PAINTED BY VANDYCK

The great range of State rooms in the south front at Wilton, completed from Inigo Jones's designs by Webb, display Palladio's principle of ordering their dimensions according to mathematical proportions and symmetry. The 'Double Cube', so called from its length being twice its height and breadth, is still one of the most magnificent rooms in England. Designed as a setting to ten of the Vandyck's great canvases painted for the 3rd and 4th Earls of Pembroke, the ceiling decoration is by Thomas de Critz. Much of the furniture was designed by Kent (c. 1735). Other rooms are no less splendid. The 8th Earl, also a leading statesman, c. 1714 acquired the Arundel marbles (collected by the Earl of Arundel, c. 1620), the Mazarin busts, gems, intaglios, and a great library. Reynolds, Richard Wilson, and Chippendale worked for his successor. Not least attractive are equestrian paintings by Morier for the 10th Earl, cavalry commander and noted horseman, c. 1770, whose entertaining letters have been recently published by Lord Herbert.

130. EAST RIDDLESDEN HALL, KEIGHLEY, YORKSHIRE

East Riddlesden Hall, Keighley, Yorkshire. (The National Trust.) The main body of East Riddlesden Hall was built for James Murgatroyd, a wealthy clothier, in 1640; the wing on the right, of which only the façade remains, was added in 1692 by the Starkie family, who lived there till about 1800, since when the house has been uninhabited. The older portion is typical of the remoter parts of Yorkshire where, at a date when Castle Ashby and Wilton were being built in Palladian classic, local masons still worked in the medieval tradition. The porch has a Gothic rose window, crockets, and battlements. Similarly, the 1692 wing is half a century earlier in style. The interior contains panelling and plasterwork of early 17th-century type.

Batemans, Burwash, Sussex. (The National Trust; *Mr W. Parrish.*) Batemans was for twenty years the home of Rudyard Kipling, round which he wrote *Puck of Pook's Hill* and *Rewards and Fairies*. The gabled, sandstone house, with tall brick chimneys, was built in 1634, by whom is unrecorded; but he was no doubt one of the local ironmasters when Burwash was a centre of the Sussex smelting industry, defunct since the 18th century. Batemans has a charming garden, and Kipling's study is preserved as he used it.

131. BATEMANS, BURWASH, SUSSEX

132. TREASURER'S HOUSE, YORK

Treasurer's House, York. (The National Trust.) Treasurer's House, beneath the shadow of York Minster, was given its present form by Sir George Young, for whom the exceptionally beautiful front with Dutch gables was added about 1610 to the Cathedral Treasurer's medieval dwelling. Parts of this earlier hall are visible in the existing house, together with much fine interior decoration of the Wren and Georgian periods. The late Mr Frank Green, who bequeathed Treasurer's House to the National Trust, began restoring it in 1898, and filled it with his particularly fine collection of period furniture, predominantly of the early 18th century.

Kew Palace, Richmond, Surrey. (The Ministry of Works.) The little red brick house with curly Dutch gables, near the entrance to Kew Gardens, is called a palace only because two Royal residences in succession were built adjoining it in the 18th century, both of which have disappeared without further trace. It was built in 1631 by Samuel Fortrey, a Flemish merchant with Dutch connections, in a style derived from the Low Countries which was fashionable in England at that date. The interior, retaining contemporary ceilings and chimney-pieces, contains a collection of animal and bird pictures, and some 18th-century furniture. It has been uninhabited since Queen Charlotte died there in 1818.

133. KEW PALACE, RICHMOND, SURREY

VI. Late Stuart, 1650–1700

The Civil War and Commonwealth temporarily arrested progress in the domestic arts. The Restoration of the Monarchy in 1660 had the effect of resolving the cleavages which had produced the catastrophe between Royalists and Republicans, Church and Puritan, country and city interests, in a spirit of tolerance and common sense. In the interests of peace and commercial prosperity, extreme views were generally discouraged, and 'enthusiasm' was checked by the spread of rational and scientific thought, symbolized by the founding of the Royal Society. It is significant that four of the best-remembered individuals of the Restoration period—Evelyn and Pepys whose diaries illuminate it so vividly, Newton and Wren whose genius shaped its achievements—were Fellows of this body, whose meetings were occasionally attended by the most rational of monarchs.

Houses and gardens strongly reflect this rationalism by their emphasis on domestic comfort and geometrical orderliness. The Italian classicism of Inigo Jones was abandoned for the more homely version of it evolved in Holland—the asylum of exiled cavaliers, linked to England by commercial rivalry and religious faith, and after 1688 by the Crown itself. Yet contact with France was also close, so that the splendours of Versailles and, much more remotely, the extravagance of Italian baroque art, are also reflected, with English restraint, in some gardens and internal decorations by the skilled craftsmen, of whom Grinling Gibbons was the most accomplished. At the end of the period, William III's Hampton Court Palace represents the fusion of French and Dutch influence with the rational style of Wren. The extremes of fashion—Puritan and baroque—at its outset are exemplified at Packwood and Astley Hall.

134. PACKWOOD HOUSE GARDEN, WITH 'THE SERMON ON THE MOUNT' IN CLIPPED YEW, c. 1650

Packwood House, Hockley Heath, Warwickshire. (The National Trust.) The old house belonged, at the outset of the Civil War, to a lawyer, John Fetherston, who, in an extant letter, describes his difficulty in deciding whether to report to Lord Northampton (of Castle Ashby), the Royalist, or Lord Broke (of Warwick), the Parliamentary representative. He avoided committing himself, and during the Commonwealth laid out the extraordinary garden (cf. Levens Hall, p. 64), which symbolizes in topiary the Sermon on the Mount: numerous obelisks of clipped yew represent the Multitude, twelve larger trees on a terrace the Apostles, and four the Evangelists adjoining the Mount, surmounted by the Master. The house, dating from 1556, has brick additions, c. 1660, and contains a fine collection of tapestry, needlework, and furniture formed by Mr Baron Ash.

135. ASTLEY HALL FROM ACROSS THE LAKE

Astley Hall, Chorley, Lancashire. (The Corporation of Chorley.) The stucco-work in the ceilings of this house, rebuilt *c.* 1670, are the most extravagant displays of baroque virtuosity to be found in England. The original Astley was a quadrangular half-timbered house, but when Richard Brooke acquired it by marriage in 1665, he rebuilt the hall range. Externally his work is characteristic of the previous generation. The hall, of two-storey height, contains the original long dining-table, as well as the richly ornamented bottom flight of the staircase. The wainscot frames a series of sepia paintings portraying principally 16th-century heroes, probably executed *c.* 1625. The compartments of the ceiling and the frieze are decorated with plaster wreaths, boys, and shields of exceptional richness, the wreaths built up of flowers and leaves each separately modelled, and the boys, modelled in the round, attached by wires. The ceiling of the drawing-room (pl. 137) is even more elaborate, every inch being encrusted with decoration, of which the central feature is composed of four large scallop-shells and two pendant boys carrying festoons, all contained within a deep floral wreath. Very large roses and other flowers fill the remainder. The craftsman responsible is not recorded, but was probably a German or Italian. Other rooms contain good plasterwork of traditional Jacobean type. Above the hall, a long gallery extends the width of the front, entirely glazed on three sides, and containing the massive and original table for the game of shuffleboard. It is a magnificent piece of carpentry, probably by the same craftsman as the staircase, and must have been built *in situ*. Astley descended to Mr Reginald Tatton, who transferred the house in 1922 to the present owners.

136. THE HALL AT ASTLEY

137. ASTLEY HALL: THE CEILING OF THE DRAWING-ROOM, c. 1670

138. THE LONG GALLERY AND ORIGINAL SHUFFLEBOARD TABLE

139. HAM HOUSE: THE ENTRANCE FRONT

Ham House, Petersham, Surrey. (The National Trust; *Ministry of Works, and Victoria and Albert Museum.*) Originally built in 1610 by Sir Thomas Vavasor as a modest country house planned as an H, Ham House became and has remained the most sumptuous example of interior decoration of the Restoration period. William Murray, 1st Earl of Dysart, redecorated the older rooms in 1637–38, also inserting the staircase. His only child, Elizabeth, secured the title of Countess of Dysart in her own right and, first wedding Sir Lionel Tollemache, allied herself with, and in 1672 married, John Maitland, member of Charles II's Cabal Ministry and subsequently Duke of Lauderdale. This formidable couple enlarged the house, with rooms filling in the south side of the H, which they decorated sumptuously, and refurnished the whole with lavish splendour. The rooms, though small in scale, and though time has somewhat tarnished their original lustre, retain most of the contents listed in the inventory of 1679.

After the Duchess's death, Ham reverted to her son, the 3rd Earl of Dysart, and continued with only slight alteration in the Tollemache family until Sir Lyonel and Mr Cecil Tollemache munificently presented the house and garden in 1948 to the National Trust. To ensure proper maintenance of the property, the Trust has leased it to the Ministry of Works, while the fabulous contents were purchased by the Government, and entrusted to the care of the Victoria and Albert Museum, which is responsible for the arrangement of the rooms.

140. THE CLOSED GATES, UNOPENED SINCE THE FLIGHT OF JAMES II

141. HAM HOUSE: THE GALLERY PANELLED IN 1639; PORTRAITS AS LISTED IN 1675

142. HAM HOUSE: THE NORTH DRAWING-ROOM, 1637

143. HAM HOUSE: THE GREAT STAIRCASE, CONSTRUCTED IN 1638

144. HAM HOUSE: THE QUEEN'S BEDCHAMBER OR 'CABAL ROOM', 1673

146. THE DUKE AND DUCHESS'S CLOSET

145. HAM HOUSE: THE MINIATURE ROOM

**147. LYME PARK: THE 1720 (LEONI) FRONT TO
THE QUADRANGLE**

Lyme Park, Disley, Cheshire. (The National Trust.) In 1346, Sir Thomas Danvers, for rescuing the Black Prince's standard at Caen and for captures effected at Crécy, was granted Lyme and the custody of Macclesfield Forest. Sir Piers Legh (see Adlington, p. 51), shortly married the knight's only daughter, so founding the race of Leghs of Lyme. And in 1946, after exactly six hundred years, the 3rd Lord Newton, Sir Piers's direct descendant, regretfully recognizing that present taxation rendered the maintenance of such a place—and such ties—impossible, transferred house and park, with considerable contents, to the National Trust.

Hunting the stag was the traditional occupation at Lyme and the origin of the house. The great park, nine miles round, and rising to 850 feet on this Pennine spur, preserves something of the old forest. The Leghs, like the Vernons of Haddon, were unambitious squires, yet the hosts of kings and queens, and content to share with their tenants and servants the good traditional life of their station.

About 1550, Sir Piers Legh VII replaced an earlier hall with the quadrangle, of which the main lines and early Renaissance gateway still stand. Then from 1650 to 1720—when the classical south front was added by the Italian architect Leoni—reconstruction was almost continuous, including the long gallery, and the acquisition of furniture. But the finest work, comprising the saloon (pl. 150), with its Grinling Gibbons carving, and the entrance hall, with Mortlake tapestries (pl. 149), are part of the 1720 alterations.

**148. AN OVERMANTEL (c. 1600) DEPICTING THE
ORIGINAL BUILDING**

149. LYME PARK: THE ENTRANCE HALL, 1720

150. GRINLING GIBBONS WORK IN THE SALOON

151. ALBURY PARK: CHIMNEYS BY AUGUSTUS WELBY PUGIN

Albury Park, Guildford, Surrey. (Helen, Duchess of Northumberland.) The associations of Albury, particularly the famous terraces and garden and picturesque park, are with the 17th century, although the house, dating from *c.* 1700, was altered by Sir John Soane in 1802 and transformed by A. W. Pugin in 1847. John Evelyn designed the canal, long terraces, and communicating tunnel beneath the hill in 1667 for Henry Howard, later 11th Duke of Norfolk, and subsequent owners have continued the tradition of choice arboriculture then initiated. The interior of the house, largely as redesigned by Soane, contains many important pictures and furniture formerly in old Northumberland House, London, together with 18th-century portraits of the banking family of Drummond.

Lullingstone Castle, Eynsford, Kent. (Lady Hart-Dyke.) Every age, from the Plantagenets to the Georges, is represented at Lullingstone, which, castle by tradition only, is now largely given over to Lady Hart-Dyke's silk farm. The little church contains an unusually rich sequence of monuments. From 15th-century Peches an heiress took the place to Sir Percyval Hart, faithful servant of four Tudor sovereigns. In the house the triptych portraits of Sir Percyval and his three sons (*c.* 1575) is noteworthy. He built the turreted brick gatehouse in front of the house, which is also of the 16th century, but was transformed about 1700. It is now predominantly of late 17th-century character, but Queen Anne's room, though fitted up for her visit, has a splendid late Elizabethan ceiling.

152. ALBURY: THE GARDEN LAID OUT IN 1667

153. LULLINGSTONE CASTLE: THE ENTRANCE FRONT AND CHURCH FROM THE GATEHOUSE

154. QUEEN ANNE'S ROOM

155. OWLETTS: FROM THE CHESTNUT AVENUE

Owletts, Cobham, Kent. (The National Trust; *Lady Baker*.)
Built in 1684 by Bonham Hayes, a prosperous yeoman of a
family farming in Cobham from at least 1517, Owletts represents how a Kentish yeoman, who in earlier times had lived in
such a house as Stoneacre (p. 46), or the hall-house in Sole
Street near Cobham (also a National Trust property), had
achieved gentry under Charles II. The richly decorated staircase and a garden laid out by Gertrude Jekyll are among the
other charms of the home of the late Sir Herbert Baker, R.A.,
who gave it to the Trust.

Gunby Hall, Skegness, Lincolnshire. (The National Trust.)
'A haunt of ancient peace.' But the much-quoted line was
written here by Tennyson, whose home, Somersby, is near-by,
and may well have been inspired by Gunby. Sir William
Massingberd, of a Saxon family settled hereabouts since the
14th century, built the Hall in 1700. The walled gardens, stable-
yard, pigeon-house, and other surroundings are as little altered
as the panelled rooms of the house. It contains, besides much
contemporary furniture, a group of portraits of the Johnson-
Boswell circle, inherited from the Doctor's friend, Bennet
Langton. Latterly Gunby was the home of Field-Marshal Sir
Archibald Montgomery-Massingberd.

156. OWLETTS: THE STAIRCASE, 1684

157. GUNBY HALL: THE MAIN FRONT

158. THE DRAWING-ROOM

159. UPTON HOUSE: THE GARDEN FRONT

Upton House, Banbury, Warwickshire. (The National Trust; *Lord Bearsted*.) Dating from *c.* 1700, in the neighbourhood of the battlefield of Edge Hill (1642), Upton contains an outstanding collection of paintings, especially interesting for its 18th-century English *genre* pictures. This was formed, and the property presented to the National Trust (1948), by the 2nd Viscount Bearsted.

Chatsworth, Bakewell, Derbyshire. (Trustees of the Chatsworth Estate.) The most famous private house of the age of Wren and the richest private treasure-house in England, the home of the Cavendishes, Dukes of Devonshire, stands in the austerely majestic landscape of the Derbyshire Peak. The formation of the building and its setting, as of the contents, extended over four centuries, and the contributions of the 18th and 19th centuries are no less notable than those of the 17th.

160. CHATSWORTH: THE VIEW DOWN THE CASCADE (c. 1700) TOWARDS THE EAST FRONT

161. CHATSWORTH: THE WEST AND NORTH FRONTS SEEN BEYOND THE BRIDGE DESIGNED BY JAMES PAINE

To view from hence the glittering Pile above,
Environ'd round with Heath, Crags, naked Hills,
Who is there but must presently conclude
That this is Paradise?

CHARLES COTTON, *Wonders of the Peak*, 1681.

In 1550, Sir William Cavendish and his wife ('Bess of Hardwick') began erecting a high quadrangular and turreted house, which was intermittently the enforced residence of Mary, Queen of Scots, 1570-81, when Lord Shrewsbury (Bess's fourth husband) was her guardian. Her 'bower' is preserved. Elizabethan Chatsworth began to be incorporated into the present building by the 1st Duke, with William Talman as architect, in 1687. At first he intended to rebuild the south front only. The east front followed, Talman being subsequently dismissed. Till 1700 the west front—that seen in the public view across the river— was still the Elizabethan entry range. But then the Duke himself, reassembling the masons, apparently erected the new façade under his own direction. The north (the present entrance) front followed under the care of Thomas Archer in 1705, and to this architect is due the baroque Cascade House on the hillside above the garden, which is seen in view in pl. 160. In the mid-18th century, Capability Brown swept away the original formal gardens, and extended the park, when James Paine designed the bridge, stables, and north entry for the 4th Duke. Wyattville remodelled the house, adding a vast north wing, 1818-39, for the 6th (Bachelor) Duke who, with his gardener Paxton, subsequently Sir Joseph and designer of the Crystal Palace, reconstructed the formal and romantic gardens as they are. But his conservatory, prototype of the 1851 Exhibition, no longer exists.

As at Hardwick, the State rooms have always been on the top floor. After Hampton Court, they afford the supreme instances of late 17th-century English decoration, including ceilings painted by Verrio, Laguerre, and Thornhill, wrought iron by Tijou, sculpture by Cibber, and wood-carving comparable to that of Grinling Gibbons by a local genius, Samuel Watson. Tapestries and furniture are of the finest quality, *c.* 1700. The superb assemblage of pictures, including the unique collection of Old Master drawings, comprise those amassed by and inherited from the 3rd (Architect) Earl of Burlington.

162. CHATSWORTH: THE STATE DRAWING-ROOM, 1689

164. THE CHAPEL; THE ALTAR-PIECE, OF DERBYSHIRE ALABASTER, BY CIBBER AND WATSON, 1690

163. CHATSWORTH: CHIMNEY-PIECE OF STATE MUSIC ROOM, 1689

165. CHATSWORTH: THE STATE BEDROOM; THE CEILING PAINTED BY SIR JAMES THORNHILL

VII. The Golden Age, 1700–1760

MARLBOROUGH'S triumphant campaigns (1704–9), the parliamentary union of England and Scotland (1707), and the accession of the Hanoverian dynasty (1715) established Britain as a continental Power. The long succeeding peace under Walpole's administration consolidated domestic prosperity and overseas trade, diffusing through the country the wealth and contentment generated during the preceding decades. An era of spiritual and intellectual equipoise ensued among men conscious of their mastery, and balancing, through human reason, their needs and resources, spiritual and physical. The age's thought was shaped by the belief that it was in men's power to recreate a perfect world on the model of that theoretically existing in the idealized classical past. The architecture and scenery reflect this dream of a humane order—which was nearly attained. The mathematical precision of the classical style gave it, in their eyes, a divine sanction, whilst a looser but no less ideal natural order might be evoked by artists in the landscapes of the countryside.

Thus this half-century that possessed many attributes of a golden age came near to resolving the dualism in English nature which has been lightly traced in these notes: the religious and intellectual, the Gothic tradition and classic learning, the formal and the free. But just as the old cleavages subsisted in the opposing régimes of Whig and Tory, so the romantic and classic impulses offered alternative routes to the ideal. In architecture, the Tory régime of Anne (1702–14) was dominated by the prestige of the aged Wren, whose mantle the genius of Sir John Vanbrugh manipulated to clothe his romantic conceptions. In Vanbrugh's extraordinary 'castles', English architecture produced a characteristic version of the continental baroque. The wealthy and enlightened Whig aristocracy, destined to rule from 1715 for fifty Georgian years, substituted for this 'enthusiasm' the reign of systematic taste founded upon rational idealism and Palladian rules. Lord Burlington assembled at his house in Piccadilly the artists who created, and Lord Shaftesbury issued the æsthetic manifesto that inspired, the Whig Arcadia: mansions in the Italian Palladio's idiom, and parks planted in the semblance of Claude's landscapes under the direction of Capability Brown, recreated the imagined scenery of a golden age.

166. BLENHEIM PALACE: THE FORECOURT AND ONE OF THE FLANKING COLONNADES

167. BLENHEIM PALACE: THE WEST FRONT AND TERRACES

Blenheim Palace, Woodstock, Oxfordshire. (The Duke of Marlborough.) Woodstock Manor had been the principal Royal hunting lodge for Wychwood Forest. The old house known as Rosamond's Bower, associated with Henry I, still stood when Queen Anne conferred the estate on John Churchill, Duke of Marlborough, to commemorate his decisive victory at Blenheim over Louis XIV of France (1704). The Duke chose Vanbrugh to be his architect, and Parliament voted the necessary but unspecified funds for the building, which began in 1705.

Vanbrugh brought to architecture, in middle life, the mind of a skilled dramatist and a powerful imagination. In place of learning, he evinced the Elizabethans' gusto for visual drama (cf. Wollaton Hall, p. 69), superb assurance and competence, and a genius for the pictorial composition of romantic shapes inspired by those of castles. Official collaboration with Wren in the Board of Works, in which he held the place of Comptroller, provided his technical training and the services of Wren's assistants and masons. But previous to 1705 he had designed only one building, though that a palace—Castle Howard.

These qualities Vanbrugh directed to the conception of the building which he and the Duke regarded as a national memorial as much as a residence, and which should combine the majesty of an historic castle with the grandeur of a Roman palace. The strong-willed and rational Duchess, however,

168. THE LONG LIBRARY

169. BLENHEIM PALACE: THE STATE ROOMS

was interested only in obtaining a country house, and friction with the architect intensified as delays in progress multiplied, culminating in her misunderstanding of his motives in seeking to preserve the ruins of Rosamond's Bower as a romantic feature of the park. On the fall of the Whig Government and of the Marlboroughs in 1712, supplies also dried up and work ceased. Building was not resumed till after the accession of George I in 1715, being completed after the Duke's death in 1722. The park and lake originally laid out by Wise were admirably redesigned about 1760 by Capability Brown, and the formal terraces, descending to the lake on the west side, were added brilliantly for the late Duke by M. Duchêne about 1930.

The exterior, with its supporting courts and towers, was finished from Vanbrugh's designs, but apart from the great hall and private apartments in the east wing, the interior was completed by Hawksmoor after the Duchess had dismissed Vanbrugh. The saloon was decorated by Laguerre; adjoining State rooms contain Brussels tapestries depicting Marlborough's victories; and Sir William Chambers revised the decoration in some instances. The long gallery filling the west side was converted to contain the great library collected by Lord Harley. The Chapel contains Rysbrack's splendid monument to the 1st Duke and Duchess.

170. IN THE GREAT HALL

171. SEATON DELAVAL: THE ENTRANCE FRONT

Seaton Delaval, Newcastle, Northumberland. (The Hon. Edward Astley.) Sublimely situated on the Northumbrian coast, Seaton Delaval was designed for Admiral Delaval about 1718, and exhibits Vanbrugh at his dramatic best. In the main block relatively few and simple elements are built up into a most forceful composition, which is led up to by an immense forecourt between arcaded wings. The impression given of a colossal stage set for tragedy is emphasized by bare interiors, gutted, but not destroyed, by fire in 1822. A surviving room is remarkable for being wainscoted in mahogany in 1720—one of the earliest uses of this wood. One of the wings contains cathedral-like stables, and the other contains the vast kitchen and three rooms with Delaval portraits, surviving furniture, etc. From the last Delavals, whose spirited and talented characters were matched by their sudden deaths, Seaton passed to the Astley family of Melton Constable, Norfolk. After further damage in the last war, the present owner has succeeded in repairing the building sufficiently for the admission of the public.

172. SEATON DELAVAL: THE APPROACH AND FORECOURT FROM THE NORTH

173. THE CATHEDRAL-LIKE STABLES

174. CLANDON PARK: THE SIDE TO THE GARDEN

Clandon Park, Guildford, Surrey. (The Earl of Onslow.) Begun in 1715 for Richard, 1st Lord Onslow, by Leoni, the Italian architect introduced to England by Lord Burlington, Clandon was one of the first big houses in the Palladian style erected by the Whig interest. The Onslows were a highly respected Whig family, established at Clandon by the Parliamentary Colonel Sir Richard Onslow in 1642, and provided no less than three Speakers to the House of Commons. The first served under Queen Elizabeth; Richard, 1st Baron, 1708–10; and his grandson Arthur, ancestor of the Earls of Onslow, 1728–61. The house is unusual in the Palladian group in being built of brick, but the interior is typical, with its large hall occupying two storeys of the front. The hall has a fine stucco ceiling in full baroque style, possibly by the Italian stuccoist Artari, and a bas-relief by Rysbrack. Similar ceilings adorn the principal rooms, several of which are lined with figured damasks and old flock papers of rich colouring, and contain fine furniture and portraits of the early 18th century. Some slight but effective changes were made in the Adam style, and among the pictures is a charming series of late Georgian pastel portraits by John Russell and Daniel Gardner. The grounds, originally formal in origin, were 'ideally' landscaped by Capability Brown.

175. SIR ROBERT WALPOLE AND SPEAKER ONSLOW IN THE OLD HOUSE OF COMMONS. PAINTED BY SIR J. THORNHILL

176. CLANDON PARK: THE HALL; BAROQUE STUCCO-WORK OF ABOUT 1720 ATTRIBUTED TO ARTARI

177. WOLTERTON HALL, NORFOLK

Wolterton Hall, Erpingham, Norfolk. (Lord Walpole.) Horatio, 1st Lord Walpole, younger brother of the great Whig Prime Minister, began building Wolterton in 1724. It was intended to be a simpler edition of Houghton, Sir Robert's palatial mansion in the same county, and was designed by Thomas Ripley, successor of Colen Campbell as architect of Houghton. The design is typical Palladian, solidly simple externally, with fine but not grandiose decoration within and interesting pictures.

178. STONELEIGH ABBEY: THE GEORGIAN FRONT

179. STONELEIGH ABBEY: EARLY GEORGIAN STUCCO DECORATION PROBABLY BY CHARLES STANLEY

Stoneleigh Abbey, Kenilworth, Warwickshire. (Lord Leigh.) On the banks of the Avon, in the heart of Warwickshire, Stoneleigh Abbey is very much a local product, despite its appearance of classic splendour. The architect was Francis Smith of Warwick, responsible for rebuilding much of that charming Georgian town, and the builder of numerous other Midland country houses. The design can be seen, however, to be provincially conservative, harking back to (say) Chatsworth, when compared with Palladian contemporaries such as Wolterton and Stourhead (pl. 182). Lord Leigh, the builder, descended from Sir Thomas Leigh, who came of a younger branch of the

Leghs of Cheshire (see Adlington, p. 51, and Lyme, p. 108), took to commerce, married his master's daughter, made a fortune, and bought the Abbey after the Dissolution. The title was conferred by Charles I for Leigh support in this predominantly Parliamentary county.

Only the gatehouse of the Abbey survives. Stately walled gardens and terraces stretch to the river. The interior of the house is one of the most magnificent of the early Georgian period, notable for the exquisite stucco reliefs on ceilings and chimney-pieces, probably by the Anglo-Swedish sculptor, Charles Stanley, and for the superb series of Leigh portraits.

180. STOURHEAD: ARCADIA IN WILTSHIRE

Stourhead, Zeals, Wiltshire. (The National Trust; *Mr H. P. R. Hoare.*) Henry Hoare, son of Sir Richard Hoare, goldsmith, banker, and Lord Mayor of London, in 1720 acquired the ancient estate of Stourton from the 13th Lord Stourton, whose ancestors are commemorated in the church. The new Palladian house was named Stourhead in distinction, and the main block was built 1720–24 from designs by Colen Campbell. The wings were added, *c.* 1800, by the builder's great-grandson, Sir Richard Colt Hoare, the historian of Wiltshire. The centre block was burnt in 1902, but was reconstructed and contains most of the original contents which well represents, with Italian paintings, family portraits, and Kent period furniture, the taste of a wealthy Whig dilettante. The library and picture gallery in the wings, which survived the fire, were furnished magnificently in the Regency style by the younger Thomas Chippendale, and display in their works of art the cultured taste of that epoch.

From 1740, Henry Hoare II transformed adjoining valleys of the downland into a unique landscape park of Arcadian scenery in the style of Claude Lorraine. It is designed round an irregular lake, so as to compose a succession of pictures in which magnificent trees and flowering shrubs frame views of the carefully sited buildings: a Roman bridge, a Pantheon, an elaborate grotto contain-

181. RYSBRACK'S 'NEPTUNE' IN THE GROTTO BY THE LAKE

182. STOURHEAD: THE HOUSE (COLEN CAMPBELL, 1721–24), BUILT FOR HENRY HOARE

ing appropriate sculpture by Rysbrack, a rustic cottage, and other classical temples designed by R. Morris and H. Flitcroft. Near the entrance, Bristol Cross (1373) was re-erected, and three miles away the Gothic Alfred's Tower commands a panorama over much of Somerset and Dorsetshire, from the Mendip Hills to the Dorset Downs, and the escarpment of Salisbury Plain.

The Stourhead landscape garden, though unique in its concentration of idyllic scenes within a relatively small compass, and in the use made of water to provide the middle distance of the views, represents a conception reflected in a large proportion of the parks surrounding country houses, and which underlay the transformation of so much of the countryside. This was that the works of great painters depicted an ideal of beauty pertaining to the mythical Golden Age, an ideal which it was the landowner's duty to restore at the same time that he improved the agriculture and forestry of his estate. The leading exponent of landscape design was Capability Brown (c. 1750–75); and among the best examples are the parks of Arundel, Blenheim, Castle Ashby, Goodwood, Longleat, Luton Hoo, West Wycombe, and Wilton.

183. THE SALOON, ADDED c. 1800

184. STOURHEAD: THE ENTRANCE HALL, 1720

185. SIR RICHARD COLT HOARE'S LIBRARY, c. 1800

186. KNOWSLEY: THE GARDEN PORTICO, 1733–37

Knowsley, Liverpool, Lancashire. (The Earl of Derby.) The seat of the Stanleys since the 14th century, the older part was built, *c.* 1485, by the 1st Earl of Derby for the reception of Henry VII, his stepson, whose victory over Richard III at Bosworth was largely due to Stanley and Lancashire support. Hereditary feudal leaders of the county, and till 1736 Kings of the Isle of Man, the Stanleys were ruined in the Royal cause during the Civil War. Knowsley, previously a rambling mixture in brick and timber, was not rebuilt in its present form, of a long, rather plain, brick mansion in the Wren tradition, till *c.* 1733 by the 10th Earl. He recorded on the portico the 'ingratitude' of Charles II in failing to make good the family's losses. The garden front, 415 feet long, was considerably improved in 1912, when the interior was largely redecorated. The very fine collection of paintings includes famous family portraits by Vandyck, Reynolds, and Romney; considerable works by Rembrandt, Claude, Poussin, Borgognone, and Hogarth; and sporting pictures illustrating the long association of the Earls of Derby with the Turf; also Victoriana connected with the 17th Earl, thrice Prime Minister.

187. HOLKHAM HALL, 1730–60: THE ENTRANCE FRONT

188.   THE SOUTH FRONT FROM THE GREAT FOUNTAIN

189. HOLKHAM: THE HALL AND THE ASCENT TO THE SALOON

190. HOLKHAM: THE LIBRARY OF LORD CHIEF JUSTICE COKE AND THOMAS, 1st EARL OF LEICESTER

Holkham Hall, Wells, Norfolk. (The Earl of Leicester.) Holkham is the outstanding monument of the Whig ideal, creating beauty and wealth where previously was only chaos. This stretch of the Norfolk coast was largely sand-dunes and salt-marsh, where 'rabbits fought for each blade of grass', till about 1730 Thomas Coke began its reclamation as a setting for his long-contemplated Roman mansion. The family's founder was Lord Chief Justice Coke, the puritanical antagonist of Francis Bacon, who, when he died in 1633, left large estates and fortune, although he 'thanked God he never gave his Body to Physic, his Heart to Cruelty, or his Hand to Corruption'. The Coke tombs are in Tittleshall Church.

His descendant, Thomas Coke, succeeded as a youth to wealth, and spent ten years on an extended Grand Tour. In Italy he encountered Lord Burlington and William Kent, with whom, before 1718, he conceived the idea of building Holkham and began acquiring the great library, paintings of the Italian school, and classical sculptures now at Holkham. For sixteen years the project was in preparation by the Burlington House circle while improvements of the estate were being forwarded. Building began in 1734. Kent was architect-in-chief for a design which, composed of selections from Palladio, Inigo Jones, and Roman models, should be regarded as the production, not of a single designer or decade, but of the experience of two centuries. The plan, of a central block with four angle pavilions (each a house in itself), follows that of Palladio's villas, but yellow brick was chosen as the material on the precept of Vitruvius. Kent laid out the park, and Nesfield the admirable formal gardens, with architectural features by William Burn, *c.* 1840.

The exterior is more grand than attractive, owing to the dun

191. HOLKHAM: THE GREEN STATE BEDROOM

brick, and partly to the substitution of plate-glass for the original sash windows. The interior, on the other hand, is not only magnificent, but escapes ornateness by the superb quality of its design and execution. In particular, the entrance hall, on the plan of a Roman basilica, leads between raised screens of columns to the ascent to the saloon on the main floor. The principal apartments have enriched ceilings after Inigo Jones, and on walls lined with red, green, or blue velvet damask, are hung superb Claudes, Poussins, and works by many notable painters. Dining-room and sculpture gallery are more purely architectural. A very agreeable balance between state and comfort is struck in the long library, running the length of one side of the main block, and containing Lord Leicester's classical MSS. and books, with those of the Lord Chief Justice.

Lord Leicester, as Thomas Coke was created in 1744, died without a surviving son in 1759, after which Holkham went to his nephew Wenman Roberts, who took the name of Coke. The latter's son succeeded to Holkham in 1776, was in 1837 created Earl of Leicester, and died in 1842—a reign of sixty-six years. He was the celebrated 'Coke of Norfolk', the friend of Charles James Fox, an ardent Whig but Protectionist, and best known of English agricultural pioneers. By widespread enclosure and forestry he converted West Norfolk from sheep-walk to rich arable and stock farming. He is said to have spent £100,000 on the farm buildings and cottages, which distinguish the estate, and raised its rent-roll from £2,000 to £20,000. His son, the 2nd Earl, lived till 1909, and the 3rd Earl till 1941.

192. WALLINGTON HALL

Wallington Hall, Cambo, Northumberland. (The National Trust; *Sir Charles Trevelyan*.) Sir Walter Blackett, an early Newcastle industrialist, bought the property from the last Fenwick of Wallington, who was later hanged for treason by William III, and began the massive granite house in 1688. (Incidentally, Fenwick was revenged, for it was on his horse White Sorral that King William was riding when it stumbled over 'the gentleman in black' and threw him so that he died.) But Wallington belongs rather to the 1740s, for it was then that Sir Walter Calverley Blackett decorated the interior and, with planting, enclosure, and village-building, transformed the bleak estate. Though Capability Brown had been born at Cambo, Sir Walter gave him only a lake to form, himself landscaping the park and designing the walled gardens, the terraces of which are peopled with delightful lead figures. And at Cambo he is said to have established a colony of Italian plasterers whose exquisite handiwork enriches the walls and ceilings. Sir Walter, too, imported from Holland, through the family business in Newcastle, the great quantities of blue-and-white porcelain seen in every room. The family portraits include an especial curiosity in Miss Sukey Trevelyan's, painted by Gainsborough and repainted by Reynolds. Students of 19th-century decoration will be interested by the central hall made in the former courtyard and painted by W. B. Scott under the eye of Ruskin. Wallington passed by inheritance to Sir Charles Trevelyan, who married the sister of Lord Macaulay; his son was Sir George Otto Trevelyan, the statesman and writer and father of Prof. G. M. Trevelyan, and of the present baronet, who in 1942 gave Wallington to the National Trust.

193. THE TERRACE IN THE WALLED GARDEN

194. WALLINGTON HALL: STUCCO DECORATION OF c. 1740 IN THE DRAWING-ROOM

195. PECKOVER HOUSE: ON THE NORTH BRINK, WISBECH

Peckover House, Wisbech, Cambridgeshire. (The National Trust.) The old inland port of Wisbech lines both banks of the River Nene with neat Georgian houses, of which this is the most important. It was built about 1720 by one of the prosperous burgesses of the town, and stands back sedately from the river-bank, with stables and coachman's house to one side, and grounds of 50 acres extending at the back. But the interior decoration was executed later, between 1730–50, for one of the Southwell family, whose wife, it is said, insisted on being in the fashion. There is a characteristic Georgian staircase with ornamented ceiling and walls, the doorways and chimney-pieces are chastely carved, and the drawing-room overmantel is a *tour de force* of rococo sculpture. The furniture and contents have remained little changed since 1777, when Jonathan Peckover, descendant of one of Cromwell's Ironsides, founded the local bank and acquired the house. Miss Alexandrina Peckover, his descendant, gave her home to the Trust in 1943.

196. ROCOCO DECORATION IN THE DRAWING-ROOM

197. GOODWOOD HOUSE, AND THE STABLES (ON THE LEFT)

Goodwood House, Chichester, Sussex. (The Duke of Richmond and Gordon.) Stag-hunting, from which fox-hunting developed, brought Charles, 2nd Duke of Richmond and Lennox, to the South Downs about 1720. (His father was one of Charles II's natural sons, by Louise de Keroualle, Duchess of Portsmouth.) For him Sir William Chambers built a hunting-box and the much more magnificent stable quadrangle. About 1800, James Wyatt began adding to the former for the 3rd Duke, on a plan intended to form a hexagon with domed towers at the corners. But only two segments (making three in all) were built, so that the resulting house is an unusual shape. The Lennoxes were a charming and handsome family—George III wanted to marry Lady Sarah, one of the 2nd Duke's daughters—and George Stubbs painted four delightful canvases of them hunting on the Downs. The grotto in the park, and the banqueting-house called after Carné the head gardener, reflect their tastes no less than the well-known race-course established near-by. The impressive rooms contain notable historic portraits and furniture of the Chippendale and Regency periods.

198. CARNÉ'S SEAT IN THE DOWNLAND PARK

199. GOODWOOD HOUSE: THE ENTRANCE HALL, BY JAMES WYATT, 1800

200. THE 3rd DUKE OF RICHMOND HUNTING AT GOODWOOD, BY GEORGE STUBBS

201. WEST WYCOMBE PARK: THE WEST PORTICO, BY ADAM AND NICHOLAS REVETT, c. 1765

202. WEST WYCOMBE PARK: THE HOUSE FROM THE SOUTH, IN THE CHILTERN LANDSCAPE, WITH THE CHURCH AND MAUSOLEUM

West Wycombe Park, Buckinghamshire. (The National Trust; *Sir John Dashwood, Bt.*) The structure of the house was built in 1707 by Sir Francis Dashwood, but it was his son, Lord Despencer, who gave it its present and unusual form between 1735 and 1765, consulting several of the leading architects of the period. He was a member of the notorious Medmenham Club, a body of free-thinking *dilettanti* whose sometimes school-boyish behaviour overshadowed their original interest in the arts. A number of portraits of members in masquerade costumes is preserved in the house. Despencer built a grand mausoleum for the members, from Adam's design, adjoining the old church (which he also rebuilt *à l'Italienne*) on the hill-top opposite. But only one member besides himself was eventually interred there. The house represents his genuine enthusiasm for the arts. Nicolas Revett and Adam both supplied designs at various times, but Despencer and his decorator, J. Donowell, evidently adapted them considerably. The double colonnade along the south front is reminiscent of Palladio, and there is an entrance portico at either end, besides a great detached archway used as a cockloft. The very beautiful landscape and surroundings of the house, including a lake and island fishing-temple, are due to Humphrey Repton, *c.* 1800. The picturesque old village and the mansion were given to the National Trust by Sir John Dashwood, who retains the contents.

203. THE TAPESTRY ROOM

204. WEST WYCOMBE PARK: THE MUSIC SALOON, c. 1760

The interiors of West Wycombe are chiefly notable for the painted decoration on the ceilings, and on the walls of the staircase. They are the work of an obscure but capable Italian named Borgnis, who copied famous originals of Raphael, the Caracci, and Guido Reni. As such they represent, in the decade of Robert Adam's rise, the end of a vogue which was at its height under Queen Anne. But by this means Lord Despencer succeeded admirably in his aim of reproducing a Palladian villa of the high Renaissance. With fine Brussels tapestries and admirable contemporary pictures and furniture, much of it in the style of Chippendale, the rooms are splendid in colouring and design.

THE last decades of the 18th century are distinguished in English architecture for the brilliant elegance associated with the genius of Robert Adam, which replaced the grand Roman manner. The shift in taste reflected the discovery of Pompeii and Athens, the domestic simplicity of the Court of the young George III (1760) with his political bias towards the Tory aristocracy, and a slow but far-reaching psychological change. The Seven Years War (1756–63) and War of American Independence (1775–81), the growth of empire and industrialism, with increasing awareness of the influence of natural forces in science, art, and conduct, unsettled the classical balance, substituting for its static ideal a disturbing consciousness of change and movement. One reaction was the beginnings of the Gothic revival and 'romanticism'; another this 'neo-classic' elegance. Both represented an as yet obscure desire to recapture the pristine virtues of an historic past which no less inspired the superb skill of the age's artists and craftsmen. The Scottish Adam, himself an instinctive romantic, applied his feeling for dynamic 'movement' in architecture to his spatial conceptions in a way not always evident from their consummate elegance of detail—derived from study of Roman excavations. The general trend continued to develop in the work of his rivals, James Wyatt and Henry Holland, and is most apparent in the increasing attention paid to the landscape setting of houses rather than to their external importance, unless the Gothic style was adopted for them.

205. CORSHAM COURT: THE GATEWAY FROM THE TOWN

206. THE FRONT, ELIZABETHAN AND GEORGIAN

Corsham Court, Chippenham, Wilts. (Lord Methuen.) Doubly a product of Cotswold wool, in that its original builder, Thomas Smythe (in 1582), and the ancestors of the Methuens, its new begetters, were Wiltshire clothiers, Corsham Court is nevertheless a great Georgian house. After many ownerships the Elizabethan house was bought in 1745 by Paul Methuen, heir of that Sir Paul who, under Queen Anne, negotiated the still-enduring Treaty with Portugal that has made port wine a national drink. The building aptly illustrates the theme of this section, in that the designer of the 1760 alterations was the landscape-architect Capability Brown, and that, instead of classicising it, he adopted the traditional style when he duplicated the original gabled wings. Since then further vicissitudes have added a side by Nash and central rooms with a tower by Bellamy (1844), though the approach from the town is still through the great Jacobean court. Recently Corsham has again been the scene of innovations: the joint occupation of the building by the owner (a well-known painter) and the West of

207. CORSHAM COURT: THE GREAT PICTURE GALLERY, 1760–72

England School of Art, whilst the State Rooms, its special glory, are shared by both parties with the public.

The picture gallery was designed by Brown. Its contents are among the most magnificent and fully documented of the period. The walls, lined with the original crimson damask (1769), are hung with Sir Paul Methuen's collection of Old Masters; at one end Vandyck's equestrian portrait of Charles I.

The unusual ceiling is the work of the Bristol plasterer, Thomas Stocking; the rich suite of chairs and settees, of Thomas Chippendale; the gilt mirrors and consoles from Adam's designs; while the Royal cabinet-makers, Vile and Cobb, supplied other pieces. Among the chief painters represented by major works are Fra Filippo Lippi, Guido Reni, Rubens, Salvator Rosa, Claude, Reynolds, and Gainsborough.

208. HATCHLANDS: A   TYPICAL MID-GEORGIAN HOUSE

Hatchlands, East Clandon, Surrey. (The National Trust ; *Mr H. Goodhart-Rendel*.) The house was built by Admiral Boscawen, commander at Louisburg and Lagos Bay (and husband of the charming letter-writer), in 1756, by an unknown architect. For its decoration, however, he turned to the young Scotsman Robert Adam, just returned from studying in Italy. The ceilings show that Adam had not yet evolved his characteristic style, but the winged figures and dolphins referring to the Admiral's fame, and crisp foliage-scrolls, closely follow excavated Roman stuccos instead of the then fashionable French rococo ornamentation. The beautiful rooms contain good paintings and furniture, both of the Boscawen epoch and of the Regency, the latter introduced by Mr Goodhart-Rendel, a Past-President of the Royal Institute of British Architects, by whom Hatchlands was inherited.

209.   PART   OF   THE   EARLIEST-KNOWN (1759) CEILING DESIGNED BY ROBERT ADAM

210. HAREWOOD HOUSE: CARR OF YORK, ROBERT ADAM, AND SIR CHARLES BARRY

Harewood House, Leeds, Yorkshire. (The Earl of Harewood.) The house was begun in 1759 by Mr Edwin Lascelles, whose ancestors had lived adjacent since the 14th century and whose father had amassed wealth in the West Indies. The original architect was John Carr of York, but almost immediately Adam was made principal partner, and the building, his first essay on the palatial scale, is essentially as he designed it. The upper storey of the wings and parapet balustrades, however, with the formal terraces, are due to Sir Charles Barry, who also altered part of the interior, in 1843. In the hall the Adam style is seen beginning to crystallize. The music room retains a carpet designed to reflect the ceiling pattern, which has medallions painted by Angelica Kauffmann. The great gallery is one of Adam's acknowledged master-pieces. Remarkable are the *trompe l'œil* drapery-festoons above the windows, carved in wood by Chippendale. Superb furniture was made for Harewood by Chippendale, but, as with John Carr, Adam's new style dominated, and permanently influenced, that master of the rococo. The collection of pictures includes many fine portraits by Reynolds, Hoppner, etc., with a small but choice collection of water-colours. The park is a beautiful example of Capability Brown's landscape, and the village, built by Carr, is of the epoch. The late Earl of Harewood married H.R.H. the Princess Royal.

211. ADAM'S HALL

212. HAREWOOD HOUSE: CHIPPENDALE'S CARVED WOOD DRAPERIES IN ADAM'S GALLERY

213. KEDLESTON HALL: THE ENTRANCE FRONT, BY JAMES PAINE, 1761

214. THE ROMAN HALL DESIGNED BY ADAM, WITH COLUMNS OF DERBYSHIRE ALABASTER

215. KEDLESTON HALL: THE SOUTH BLOCK, BY ROBERT ADAM

Kedleston Hall, Derby. (Viscount Scarsdale.) The forebears of Nathaniel Curzon, 1st Lord Scarsdale, had lived at Kedleston since the reign of Henry I, when he, a man of informed tastes and considerable means, began to rebuild the house about 1760. The old village that stood in front of it was re-erected at a more discreet distance. Matthew Brettingham made the first designs, on the same plan as Holkham, but was replaced by James Paine, leading country-house architect of the mid-century, who completed the entrance front and wings in 1761. Adam was first engaged to decorate the interior, but shortly replaced Paine as

architect, and completely revised the design of the south elevation. With its wings, which were never built, this was designed to demonstrate Adam's conception of 'movement'—a quality for which he admired Vanbrugh. This domed and columned front, approached by curving steps and enriched with carefully placed sculpture, does, although incomplete, forcefully display Adam's power as an architect when compared with the static north elevation. It was, indeed, the most complete embodiment of his conception that he was destined to realize.

The monumental interiors of Kedleston (1760–70) surpass

216. KEDLESTON HALL: LOOKING FROM THE DOMED SALOON TO THE HALL

anything that Adam was to produce subsequently, except Syon. Nowhere was he able to such an extent to use genuine materials or to follow so closely the spirit of Roman buildings that he had studied. The quality of 'movement' is conveyed by the relationship and contrasting forms of the rooms. The vast hall (pl. 214), with twenty columns of green-veined alabaster and stuccos by Joseph Rose, is most impressive, and leads into the circular saloon, which recalls the Pantheon. The living-rooms flanking these are of restrained magnificence. The dining-room, with Zucchi's ceiling-panels, contains paintings by Claude, Zucch-arelli, etc.; the drawing-room, a remarkable suite of furniture embodying mermaids, made by Seddon to Adam's designs. The chimney-pieces, by Spang and Wilton, are in some cases inlaid with bluejohn spar. Of numerous important pictures, Rembrandt's 'Daniel interpreting Nebuchadnezzar's Dream' is perhaps the most notable. As usual in these large Georgian houses, one of the wings provides self-contained accommodation for the owner. The adjacent church contains a series of Curzon monuments culminating in that of Marquess Curzon of Kedleston, Viceroy of India, and Foreign Secretary.

217. SYON HOUSE: THE EXTERIOR PRESERVES THE STRUCTURE OF THE CONVENT FOUNDED BY HENRY V

Syon House, Brentford, Middlesex. (The Duke of Northumberland.) After the dissolution of the convent, Syon was occupied by Protector Somerset and John Dudley, Duke of Northumberland, before being granted by James I to Henry Percy, 9th Earl of Northumberland, for whom Inigo Jones made alterations. In 1762, the 1st Duke commissioned Adam to fit up the apartments in a magnificent manner. Their effect derives as much from his brilliant contrasting of shapes and colouring as from their great intrinsic beauty. From the hall, richly Roman in white and black, we enter the superb anteroom glowing with subdued gold and colour in marble, scagliola, and Joseph Rose's masterly reliefs. In the succeeding dining-room, ivory and gold predominate. Next, the drawing-room, illustrated in colour in the frontispiece, is hung with crimson silk, has the specially woven Moorfields carpet of reds, golds, and blues, while the gilded ceiling contains *paterœ* of small reliefs with red and blue grounds painted by Angelica Kauffmann. This leads to the exquisite long gallery, originally Jacobean, but redecorated by Adam in pastel shades, with inset paintings, to a design as satisfying in perspective as in detail. Succeeding rooms in the circuit round the former cloister contain the historic collection of Percy family portraits from the Tudor period onwards. (See also Alnwick Castle, p. 20, and Albury Park, p. 110.)

218. ADAM'S ENTRANCE HALL

219. SYON HOUSE: THE ANTEROOM; ANTIQUE GREEN MARBLE COLUMNS AND GILDED RELIEFS

220. SYON HOUSE: THE LONG GALLERY

221. SYON HOUSE: THE DINING-ROOM; THE COLOUR SCHEME IS IVORY AND GOLD

222. KENWOOD: ADAM'S LIBRARY DESIGNED FOR LORD MANSFIELD

Kenwood, Hampstead, London. (The London County Council.) In 1767 Lord Chancellor Mansfield commissioned Adam to add wings to an older house. The finest room is the library, which is one of the most satisfying of Adam's interiors.

In 1927 the Earl of Iveagh bequeathed Kenwood to the nation, together with his celebrated collection of paintings. Rembrandt, Vermeer, and Hals are outstandingly represented, and the 18th-century English school is nowhere more delightfully displayed.

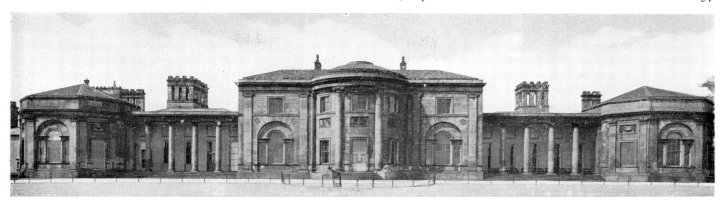

223. HEATON PARK: THE SOUTH FRONT, 1772

224. THE ETRUSCAN ROOM AT HEATON PARK

Heaton Park, Prestwick, Manchester. (Manchester Corporation.) Thomas Egerton, 1st Earl of Wilton, in 1772 employed James Wyatt to reconstruct the house built of brick by his father. In the previous year, Wyatt, aged twenty-five, had captivated London by his simplified version of Adam's neo-classic manner, which critics were beginning to find over-elaborate: awareness of ancient Greek art, and the growing interest in fabricated as against hand-produced articles were among the contributory causes of this change of taste. At Heaton, exemplifying the latter trend, the capitals of the columns are of cast iron and the sculpture of artificial cast stone. Wyatt's internal decoration is 'prettier' and slighter than Adam's, owing much to Hellenistic models. However, the room in the cupola on the south front is exquisitely decorated by Biagio Rebecca in the Etruscan style. Manchester Corporation acquired house and park in 1901, but without the contents.

225. OSTERLEY PARK: ADAM'S PORTICO

Osterley Park, Middlesex. (The National Trust.) Two families of
merchant princes at an interval of two hundred years were responsible
for this notable house, now on the outskirts of London. Though
superbly decorated within and cleverly remodelled by Adam for Sir
Robert Child, the house is that built round a courtyard in about 1570
by Sir Thomas Gresham, the founder of the Royal Exchange. The
building is therefore contemporary with Longleat and Burghley. It was
bought in 1711 by Sir Francis Child, son of a Wiltshire clothier, and
founder of Child's Bank (cf. the Hoares of Stourhead, p. 128). Wan-
stead House, Essex, designed by Colen Campbell but demolished in
1822, was the principal Child establishment till the process of reconstruction by Adam (1761–73) made Osterley 'the palace of palaces' as
Horace Walpole called it. Instead of entirely rebuilding as first intended,
the first storey of the old house was made the principal floor, the courtyard was vaulted over to form a raised internal court, and the main front
pierced by the spectacular Grecian portico or 'propeileum' approached
by a grand flight of steps.

Adam nowhere directed greater care to internal decoration than at
Osterley, where he also designed most of the exquisite furniture. His
work here falls into two periods, 1766–73 and 1775–77. Of the former
are the hall, with reliefs like those by Rose at Syon (pl. 219), the
library where panels by Angelica Kauffmann surmount architectural
bookcases, and the dining-room with panels by Zucchi and festoons

226. IN THE ENTRANCE HALL

227. OSTERLEY PARK: THE LIBRARY, DESIGNED BY ADAM, 1766

of flowers on the ceiling. The drawing-room, with a coloured ceiling of an early Adam type, has its original carpet by Moore. In the later rooms Adam's decoration is of that slighter, linear, non-architectural character usually associated with his name, but which caused some contemporaries to take exception to him and to transfer their patronage to Wyatt. As rooms, however, they are of much beauty: the tapestry room, hung and furnished with *rose-du-Barri* Gobelins signed by Nielson 1775, the painted Etruscan Room, and the State Bedroom with its throne-like bed.

The furniture throughout is of sumptuous elegance, mostly designed by Adam, from magnificent gilt mirrors and veneered commodes to such exquisite trifles as incense-burners. A long gallery, to which Adam contributed little in comparison to that at Syon, is hung with the Child family portraits, including a series by Romney, and a continental collection typical of the period.

Osterley is associated with one of the most celebrated of runaway matches, when Robert Child's beautiful daughter eloped to Gretna with the handsome 10th Earl of Westmorland in 1782. Their daughter took Osterley to her husband, the 5th Earl of Jersey, and lived, famous in society, till 1867. The 9th Earl gave this superb mansion to the National Trust in 1949, when the furniture was bought by the Victoria and Albert Museum, and the whole leased by the Ministry of Works, which has recently carried out extensive repairs.

228. THE STATE BED, DESIGNED BY ADAM, c. 1775

229. OSTERLEY PARK: THE ETRUSCAN ROOM, c. 1775

230. OSTERLEY PARK: GOBELINS TAPESTRIES BY NIELSON, 1775

231. BUSCOT PARK: A GEORGIAN HOUSE RECENTLY RESTORED

Buscot Park, Faringdon, Berkshire. (The National Trust; *Lord Faringdon*.) Built *c.* 1775 from his own designs by E. L. Townsend, Buscot was, and is now again, a charming building of the Age of Elegance. But 19th-century additions, including a top-heavy roof, concealed its character. This was removed and the house reduced in size in 1938, the wings now forming a detached dwelling and a small theatre (decorated by the Earl of Huntingdon). The rooms, notable for their Wyatt-type ceilings and chimney-pieces, contain some first-rate pictures (Gains-borough, Reynolds, etc.) and furniture of the period. The saloon is especially remarkable for the picture-sequence 'The Sleeping Beauty' (1871) by the Pre-Raphaelite painter, Sir E. Burne-Jones. The late Lord Faringdon (then Mr Alexander Henderson) acquired them, and the artist, when staying with William Morris near-by at Kelmscott (see p. 81), designed the setting of the panels. The work constitutes one of the most extensive of the Pre-Raphaelite school, and harmonizes well with choice satinwood furniture.

232. THE 'SLEEPING BEAUTY' ROOM, BY SIR E. BURNE-JONES

233. ATTINGHAM PARK: LATE GEORGIAN ELEGANCE

Attingham Park, Shrewsbury. (The National Trust; *The Shropshire County Council*.) Built by Noel Hill, 1st Lord Berwick, in 1784, from designs by a little-known Scottish architect, George Stewart, with an important picture gallery inserted by Nash in 1807. The park and lake are excellent typical productions of the landscape-architect Humphrey Repton. Stewart's building, with its tall slender columns and colonnades, well illustrates the elegance of the late 18th century, and its internal decoration is particularly attractive in the style of Wyatt. The furniture, and many of the pictures, were collected by the 3rd Lord Berwick when Minister at Naples—notably the Louis XVI and Empire furnishings of the drawing-room, much of it signed pieces. The paintings, mostly contained in the picture gallery, comprise works by Caravaggio, Salvator Rosa, the Venetian, Veronese, and Spanish schools, and a series of landscapes by Philip Hackaert (*c.* 1795), a friend of Goethe. Given to the National Trust by the 8th Lord Berwick, part of the house is used by the College of Adult Education.

234. THE DRAWING-ROOM

235. ATTINGHAM PARK: THE HALL OF GREY SCAGLIOLA

Althorp, Northampton. (The Earl Spencer.) Althorp is one of the best examples among country houses of the work of Henry Holland, the Prince Regent's first architect. But it is also one of the great historic houses of England, and dates structurally from *c*. 1580. Sir John Spencer, its builder, was great-grandson of a Warwickshire yeoman, who founded the family's fortunes in Cotswold sheep and wool, and father of the cavalier 1st Lord Sunderland. The 2nd Earl of Sunderland, ambassador and politician, transformed the house in the late 17th century, hanging the long gallery with Stuart portraits, and filling in the Elizabethan forecourt with the grand staircase. The 3rd Earl, *c*. 1733, gave the exterior its present shape, and decorated the two-storeyed hall with enormous hunting-pieces by John Wooton. Having married the second daughter of the Duke of Marlborough, his son, the 5th Earl, in 1733 succeeded to that Dukedom, and many Marlborough treasures are thus at Althorp, which passed to his nephew, created 1st Earl Spencer. The 2nd Lord Spencer in 1788 engaged Holland for drastic renovations necessitated by the condition of the old house.

Holland refronted the walls in white brick and stone, and also redesigned the park. Retaining the principal old rooms intact, he formed the suite along the west front which, comprising

236. ALTHORP: HOME OF THE SPENCERS SINCE THE 16th CENTURY

237. ALTHORP: THE PICTURE GALLERY, LATE 17th CENTURY

dining-room, drawing-room and long library, represents admirably the last phase of the Age of Elegance. Holland's style, influenced by French Louis XVI taste, achieves an exquisite simplicity, employing the minimum of enrichment needed to give colour to rooms which charm by their perfect proportions and grace.

The collection of pictures is most famous for its wonderful series of portraits by Sir Joshua Reynolds, but is also extremely rich in 17th-century painting. The series of family portraits painted before the Civil War no doubt included many of the great group of Vandycks. The 2nd Earl of Sunderland (*temp.* Charles II) was a discerning collector, to whom are due the Rubens, Dutch portraits, further Vandycks, and notable Dobson and Lely portraits. The collection of Sarah, Duchess of Marlborough, and the landscapes, etc., acquired for Spencer House, are now at Althorp. The Spencer tombs at Great Brington are among the finest applications of 17th-century sculpture.

238. THE LONG LIBRARY, 1790

239. ALTHORP: THE HALL, DECORATED c. 1733, AND LINED WITH HUNTING-SCENES BY WOOTON

240. AYNHO PARK: THE GARDEN FRONT

Aynho Park, Banbury, Northamptonshire. (Mr Richard Cartwright.) An ancient house destroyed in the Civil War was replaced in 1662 by the existing building, in the Inigo Jones style, on three sides of an entrance court. John Cartwright, the owner and defender for Parliament, obtained £10,000 in compensation from the Earl of Northampton, its besieger. About 1795 the south front was extended to 220 feet with wings added by Sir John Soane, who also redecorated much of the interior in his severe but still elegant style. The collection of pictures, very extensive and interesting, comprises a remarkable series by Murillo, works by Veronese, Rubens, Poussin, Italian baroque masters, and the Dutch School, notably van der Velde and Backhuisen. The family portraits include a delightful Hogarth, Gainsborough, and several Benjamin Wests, in addition to a particularly interesting collection of 17th-century portraits. The oriental porcelain is notable, as are the French and Italian furniture and Sèvres porcelain.

241. THE SOANE DRAWING-ROOM, *c.* **1795**

THE decline of the country house as a social organism began in the 19th century as the result of many factors. The first Reform Bill (1832) began to diminish the landed interest's political power; the repeal of the Corn Laws (1846) finally subordinated the economic interests of agriculture, on which rested the prosperity of landed estates, to the needs of a predominantly urban population; and the coming of the railways did away with the self-sufficiency which had remained one of the chief purposes of country houses since the era of feudal castles. The very great majority of places continued in being, however, as this partial survey has shown, and large numbers of country houses continued to be built, because the English way of life remains based upon the amenities of the countryside. The immense wealth of Victorian England indeed added the families of innumerable manufacturers, merchants, and administrators to the ranks of the landed gentry, who found in local affairs and democratic politics scope for their energies amply compensating for the old territorial privileges. The aristocracy continued, till the dawn of the present century, the most fertile source of statesmanship, and such houses as Hatfield, Chatsworth and Knowsley, Cliveden and Hughenden, saw the reality of power undiminished.

Amid the century's social and moral chaos, the country house may be said to have constituted the most enduring and least affected element in the structure of society. Nevertheless, the new houses erected (and the many enlarged or rebuilt) plainly reflect that confusion of values which brought with it a corresponding confusion in the arts. The 19th-century's inventive force went unconsciously into the 'science' of engineering. In architecture, the dominant criterion of designs in whatever style was their picturesqueness. This aspect had been intermittently potent since the Tudor and Elizabethan epochs, had predominated in Vanbrugh's baroque, and been recognized by Adam, while it had developed an æsthetic of its own in landscape architecture. Henceforth, whether acknowledged or not, picturesque irregularity of outline and plan, and harmony of house with setting, whether its style was Gothic, Italian, or old English, was the underlying aim. The movement initiated by William Morris (c. 1870) envisaged a modern architecture, but was diverted by its founder's passion for the virtues of the Middle Ages and honest craftsmanship into the loving restoration, or imitation, of ancient buildings (see Kelmscott, p. 81, and Wightwick, p. 171). In garden design the picturesque motive produced many admirable results, particularly in the early 20th century. The Edwardian era applied much connoisseurship and wealth to resurrecting in its houses the Wren tradition, and assembling catholic collections of works of art.

242. REGENCY LANDSCAPE: DINTON HOUSE, WILTSHIRE

Dinton House, Salisbury. (The National Trust.) The view of Dinton House from the Salisbury–Wincanton road is worth seeing as representing in its design and landscape setting a country house of the last phase of the classical tradition in England. It was built in 1808–18, in the Grecian style, by Sir J. Wyattville, better known for his Gothic reconstruction of Windsor Castle, for the Wyndham family. In the village, Hyde's House, birthplace of the Cavalier Earl of Clarendon, is a small Tudor house belonging to the National Trust but not open to the public; Little Clarendon is a stone Tudor house of some interest (National Trust); and Lawes Cottage was the birthplace of the Jacobean musician.

243. HUGHENDEN MANOR, THE HOME OF BENJAMIN DISRAELI, 1847-81

244. LORD BEACONSFIELD'S DRAWING-ROOM

Hughenden Manor, High Wycombe, Buckinghamshire. (The National Trust.) Hughenden stands high among the Chiltern Hills, overlooking a charming park, which also contains the church where Disraeli is buried. The house is really Georgian, *c.* 1780, of red brick with blue headers, but was ingeniously altered in 1847 by the architect E. B. Lamb to present the Tudor appearance required by the young Disraeli with his romantic passion for the English tradition. The interior is of much charm. Some good Georgian features survive, notably in Disraeli's library, but the rooms predominantly reflect his own somewhat exotic taste and that of the 1840s. The drawing-room, hung with rich blue damask, contains principally French and rococo furniture; in a large and undeniably ugly dining-room are interesting mid-Victorian portraits. A small room is filled with early 19th-century sketches and drawings of his friends collected by Disraeli, and his study is as he left it. The statesman's son, Major Coningsby Disraeli, lived at Hughenden till 1936, when Mr W. H. Abbey generously purchased the house, contents, and park for preservation. It was opened to the public in 1949.

245. CLIVEDEN: THE RIVER FRONT

Cliveden, Taplow, Buckinghamshire. (The National Trust.) In a magnificent position above the Thames, Cliveden has been a famous country house since first built for George Villiers, Duke of Buckingham. When Frederick Prince of Wales was tenant of Cliveden in 1755 the song 'Rule Britannia' was first given, in a masque by James Thomson and Dr Arne. Twice burnt and rebuilt, the present house was designed for the Duke of Sutherland in 1850 by Sir Charles Barry, who adapted the original design to the demand for an Italian *palazzo*. This character is emphasized by the impressive formal gardens, adorned with admirable sculptures from the Villa Borghese, laid out in the '90s for the 1st Viscount Astor. The interior, redecorated in the Renaissance style (architect, J. L. Pearson), contains a catholic collection of pictures.

A-la-Ronde, Exmouth, Devon. (Miss M. L. B. Tudor.) This peculiar circular house, erected by two artistic spinsters and filled with their curious handicrafts, was built about 1800. The Misses Jane and Mary Parminter, of good Devon middle-class stock, travelled abroad for ten years sight-seeing, then decided to continue their association at Exmouth in a house which they designed to incorporate certain features of the Byzantine Church of S. Vitale, Ravenna. There is indeed an octagonal hall 60 feet high, and its upper surfaces are encrusted with mosaics, but executed in feathers and shells. Shells and grottoes fill fireplaces, there are pictures executed in sand and seaweed, furniture either hand-painted or of doll's-house size, and rows of family silhouettes.

246. A-LA-RONDE: FEATHER MOSAICS IN THE OCTAGONAL HALL

247. KNEBWORTH HOUSE

Knebworth House, Hertfordshire. (Mr C. F. and Lady Hermione Cobbold.) The romantic creation of Edward Bulwer-Lytton, 1st Lord Lytton, and famous Victorian novelist, Knebworth none the less incorporates one wing of the original Tudor mansion of the Lyttons. As rebuilt by him about 1843, the house is in the Tudor style, which also attracted Disraeli and inspired the Houses of Parliament. The interior contains original woodwork, tapestry, and furniture—much of the latter 'made up' to conform with the period's romantic conceptions—together with family and other portraits of authentic merit.

Wightwick Manor, Wolverhampton, Staffordshire. (The National Trust; *Sir Geoffrey Mander*.) Built in the half-timber technique, 1887–93, from designs by Edward Ould for Mr S. T. Mander, Wightwick exemplifies the influence of Pre-Raphaelite ideals on design. The craftsmanship is admirable, and the decoration, representative of the most informed taste of the period, includes wall-papers by William Morris. The notable collection of pictures comprises water-colours by Ruskin, drawings by Burne-Jones (cf. Buscot, p. 162), and Pre-Raphaelite paintings lent by Miss Rosetti Angeli.

248. WIGHTWICK MANOR: THE HALL

249. POLESDEN LACEY FROM THE LAWNS

Polesden Lacey, Dorking, Surrey. (The National Trust.) In its beautiful downland setting and filled with notable works of art, Polesden Lacey retains completely the atmosphere of a great Edwardian hostess's country home—down to the signed photographs of Royalties in silver frames upon her writing-table. The modest late-classic house was erected in 1824 by Thomas Cubitt, the contractor who built much of Regency London, on the site of a Carolean one owned for a time by Richard Brinsley Sheridan, who laid out parts of the picturesque garden. The house was remodelled and the gardens much extended by the Hon. Mr and Mrs Ronald Greville in 1906. The eclecticism of Edwardian taste is displayed within by the tasteful *mélange* of rococo gilding, Italian and Wren panelling, French marquetry furniture, Chinese porcelain, jade and bronzes and cushioned comfort. Nevertheless, the collection of pictures is of the first order. It includes early Flemish portraits, outstanding works by the English 18th-century school, and the group of Raeburn portraits culminating in the 'Patterson Children'.

250. RAEBURN PORTRAITS IN THE DINING-ROOM

251. LUTON HOO: THE ADAM FRONT AS ALTERED IN 1903

Luton Hoo, Luton, Bedfordshire. (Maj.-Gen. Sir Harold Wernher, Bt.) The late Sir Julius Wernher, one of the creators of the Rand Goldfields, in 1903 bought the house, originally designed by Adam for the Earl of Bute, George III's Prime Minister, and set in a noble Capability Brown park. The house was enlarged and redecorated for Sir Julius by Messrs. Mewes & Davis, architects of the Ritz Hotel, in much the same refined Edwardian taste. The new owner was a collector of works of art on the scale of Pierpoint Morgan, and it is of these, perhaps the most varied and valuable private collection in England, that Sir Harold Wernher has now composed a museum which occupies the half of the house open to the public. Almost every department of art is very well represented. The picture collection ranges from the Primitive Schools to the Dutch and English. The Ludlow Collection of English porcelain occupies three rooms; the displays of medieval ivories and Renaissance bronzes, tapestries, silver, and jewels are remarkable; and a room is devoted to paintings and relics of Sir Harold's celebrated race-horse Brown Jack.

252. THE LOUIS XIV DINING-ROOM

**253. PLAS NEWYDD: THE DINING-ROOM DECORATED
BY REX WHISTLER**

Plas Newydd, Anglesea. (The Marquess of Anglesea.) Henry William
Paget, Earl of Uxbridge, who commanded the Allied cavalry and lost a
leg at Waterloo, was, in recognition, created Marquess of Anglesea and
remembered by his family as Uncle One-leg. About 1810 he had engaged James Wyatt to remodel Plas Newydd, which stands on the
southern shore of the island near the end of the Victoria Bridge, and
looking across the strait to the mountains of Snowdonia. The house, a
charming example of Wyatt's 'Gothick', contains the Paget heirlooms
going back to Tudor times and formerly at Beaudesert in Staffordshire,
the family's original abode, now demolished. The most distinctive
feature, however, is the room decorated in 1937 by the late Rex Whistler, artist and designer of genius, who was killed in Normandy leading
his company soon after D-Day. The painting is a romantic version of
the view from the windows—a prospect across a gulf to an imaginary
city lying below a range of mountains—and is an enchanting pastiche
of every place Rex Whistler enjoyed: Venice, Brighton, Dublin, Wren's
London, Rome, Amalfi. Its nostalgic evocation of Renaissance civilization may fitly end this survey of English country houses, to which,
however, are appended two outstanding gardens.

254. A DETAIL OF THE DECORATION

255. HIDCOTE BARTRIM: ONE OF THE GARDEN 'ROOMS'

Hidcote Bartrim, Chipping Campden, Gloucestershire. (The National Trust.) This garden is the creation during the last fifty years of Mr Lawrence Johnstone. Set high on the Cotswolds, the spot had no natural advantages and no natural feature, except a fine cedar tree in the angle of the old house. Taking this as the pivot of the plan, and making a virtue of the necessity for shelter, Mr Johnstone devised a type of garden which adopted elements from both the formal and naturalistic kinds. A long grass alley, aligned on the cedar and flanked by deep borders backed by hedges, is its spine, off which open a succession of 'rooms' devoted to particular associations of plants. By this means protection from winds, specialized conditions, and controlled visual effects were secured. Many uncommon plants have been naturalized by this means.

256. THE GARDENS AT BODNANT AND THE VIEW TO THE SNOWDON MOUNTAINS

Bodnant, Near Llandudno, Denbighshire. (The National Trust; *Lord Aberconway*.) The Bodnant domain is a gardened mountain valley comprising natural woodland, water, and hillside, besides architectural layout on a grand scale, the whole in a magnificent scenic setting. Its makers over the last seventy years have been Lord Aberconway and his mother, whilst a majority of the choice trees were planted by the 1st Lord Aberconway, his father. The wooded glen in the bottom and its sides are devoted principally to an immense range of the genus azalea (with which is included *rhododendron*), with massed primulas and aquatics bordering the stream. Immediately below the house (whence the photograph is taken) a series of broad terraces descends the slope, their rough stone walls clothed with the widest range of flowering shrubs. The lowest terrace is largely filled by a formal canal, at one end of which is erected a two-storeyed Georgian gazebo.